THE ACTS
OF THE APOSTLES

with Introduction by

Henry Wansbrough OSB

All booklets are published thanks to the
generous support of the members of the
Catholic Truth Society

CATHOLIC TRUTH SOCIETY
PUBLISHERS TO THE HOLY SEE

Contents

The Jerusalem Bible translation

The Jerusalem Bible was first published in 1966. It was produced by a team of distinguished English scholars (including J.R.R. Tolkien), working under Alexander Jones. It made available for English readers the findings of the French *Bible de Jérusalem* published a decade earlier by the famous French biblical school in Jerusalem, the first Catholic Bible edition to incorporate all the advances of modern biblical study. The Jerusalem Bible was the first translation of the whole Bible into modern English, and as such has maintained its status as authorised for use in the liturgy.

❧ INTRODUCTION ❧

Luke's first volume, his Gospel, has brought the reader to
the climactic point of the Resurrection and the first story
of the proclamation of the Good News of the Risen Christ
to the disciples on the road to Emmaus. Starting from the
hinge-point of Jerusalem, the second volume shows the
Good News spreading to the ends of the earth, that is, in
Jewish parlance of the time, to Rome. All the criteria of
style, vocabulary, literary structure and theology leave no
doubt that this work is a second volume authored by the
same mind and pen as the Gospel of Luke (a particularly
cogent example is the similarity of the stories of the
disciples on the road to Emmaus in *Luke* 24:13-33 and the
instruction of the Ethiopian official in *Acts* 8:26-40). The
story reads like an adventure-story, with plenty of trials
leading to the freeing of the hero, dangerous journeys and
ordeals, escapes from prison, shipwrecks - just the stuff of
the novels of the time. As a teenager it was the first story I
was given to read in Greek. Yet it is serious history. Luke
has done his research and makes no mistake about the
complex and varied political circumstances of the Greco-
Roman Empire of the eastern mediterranean where Paul
was spreading the message. Many of the details of route,
distance and lodgings seem to go back to a diary or log-
book kept by the travellers. There are some passages
where the writer suddenly bursts into the first person ('We

set sail...'), which suggests that the author or his source was actually travelling with Paul. Yet there is a marked difference in tone between the travel diary and the 'set pieces', such as the evangelisation of the Ethiopian official (8:26-40), the miraculous release of Peter (12:1-19) and of Paul (16:25-40). These are made memorable by Luke's imagination, lively dialogue and wit (cf. 19:13-17). Perhaps the masterpiece of story-telling is the account of the shipwreck in 27:9-44.

An important proportion of the book also consists of speeches or sermons, which function not only as examples of Christian evangelisation, but also to comment on the action. It was a convention of ancient history-writing to express editorial comment in the form of speeches put into the mouth of authoritative characters. Thus Peter's speech in 2:14-36 explains the significance of the events of Pentecost, and Stephen's speech in 7:1-53 marks the turning-point of the Christian mission away from Jerusalem. Paul also gives two great exemplary speeches, one in the synagogue at Antioch, an example of Christian preaching to the Jews (13:17-41) and the other before the Areopagus of Athens, an example of Christian preaching to the gentiles (17:22-31). Luke also skillfully brings out his message by the use of Old Testament models, and indeed other secular literary models. Thus the vocation of Paul (9:3-19) is narrated in terms of the conversion of Heliodorus, the persecutor of God's People

in *2 Maccabees* 3, and Paul's interventions during the
fateful shipwreck-voyage (27:21-26, 33-36; 28:3-6) show
him to be a prophet like Jonah.

Plan of the book of Acts

The scheme of the book follows the spread of the gospel
to the ends of the earth, and it begins with a picture of the
ideal Christian community at Jerusalem. The Twelve bear
witness to the Resurrection of Jesus even to the point of
persecution by the Sanhedrin, despite the protestations of
Gamaliel (perhaps the most respected Rabbi of the time)
that if this movement is from God it will be indestructible.
The account is interspersed with summaries which show
the life of the community, united in heart and in prayer,
faithful to the Temple and to the breaking of bread,
generous and sharing their possessions. Luke often works
by parallels (in the Infancy Narrative of the gospel, the
parallel between John the Baptist and Jesus). So by the
coming of the Spirit at the beginning of the mission, and
by the parallel between the miracles of the apostles with
those of Jesus he shows that the community carries on in
the Spirit the life of Jesus while he was on earth. This
period comes to an end with the great speech of Stephen
and with his martyrdom (chapter 7), again parallel to the
martyrdom of Jesus. Stephen's speech marks the finding
that despite being given a second chance, the Jews are still
stiff-necked like their ancestors.

With this persecution begins the second phase, the spread of the gospel to Samaria (8:4-8) and the coastal region of Palestine. Now occurs that significant event, the reception into the community of the first gentile, the centurion Cornelius (Ch.10). So significant is it that it is related three times, always with the emphasis that it is the work, not of Peter, but of the Holy Spirit. As such, the apostolic community at Jerusalem give it their seal of approval. Overlapping with this comes the other event of such significance that it is narrated three times [once on the road to Damascus (Ch.10), once in Paul's speech in the Temple (22:6-11), once in his defence before "King Agrippa (26:12-13)"], the vocation of Saul the persecutor to become Paul, the apostle of the gentiles.

Then begins - again with a carefully-drawn parallel between Peter and Paul - the advance of the gospel to the ends of the earth. The problems of Jews and gentiles living and worshipping together, raised by the first 'Christian' community at Antioch (15:1-2) and by Paul's first missionary journey as an emissary of this community, are settled by the 'Council of Jerusalem' (15:5-21) (an account for which Luke seemingly combines at least two different meetings of the church). Then Paul sets out, under the insistent guidance of the Spirit, on two more journeys, carrying the gospel first to Asia Minor (Ch.16) and then to Greece (Ch.17). Finally Paul returns to Jerusalem (Ch.21), where he is taken prisoner, stands trial before two successive governors at Caesarea (Ch. 24), and appeals to Caesar in Rome (25:1-12). After an adventurous journey he reaches the capital (28:14), where he is greeted by the Christian brothers, and finally has the opportunity to proclaim the gospel at 'the ends of the earth'. With this the story has reached its goal and comes to an end, leaving us no further information about Paul's subsequent history.

The Message of the book

The dominant theme of the book is the guidance of the Spirit. Just as Jesus' mission begins with the descent of the Spirit at his baptism, so the mission of his apostles begins with the descent of the Spirit at Pentecost. Thenceforth we are constantly reminded that the ministers of the community are filled with the Spirit (6:3; 7:55; 10:19), that the counsels and decisions of the community are inspired by the Spirit (10:44; 13:4; 15:28), that the missionaries are directed in every detail by the Spirit (16:6), and that the Spirit controls history to the extent of prophesying what will happen to them in the future (20:23; 21:11).

This theme of the guidance of the Spirit enables Luke to stress continually the unity of the first community, not only in the ideal community of Jerusalem but throughout the activity of the Christians. Paul returns constantly to Jerusalem, the focus of unity, as though to check for approval of his activity. A critical eye may discern that the appointment of the seven 'deacons' in fact conceals a

fair amount of quarrelling between Hebrew and
Hellenistic disciples, which is deliberately understated by
Luke. There is no word of the stand-up row between
Peter and Paul at Antioch (*Ga* 2:11-14), or of Paul's
apprehension about his reception on his final journey to
Jerusalem (*Ac* 21:19). Luke does not wish any wrinkle to
disfigure the fair face of the Church.

One of Luke's especial concerns is the salvation of the
Jews. How is it that the Chosen Race, formed so long by
God's promises, eventually failed to respond? In the
Gospel Luke had insisted that, while the leaders were
opposed to Jesus, the mass of the people gave him a
favourable reception; the child was to be 'the glory of
your people Israel' (*Lk* 2:32). Now, even though the
official representatives repeatedly reject the message,
Luke insists that large numbers at Jerusalem were
converted (*Ac* 2:41; 4:4). On three occasions, in each
stage of his mission, in Asia Minor, in Greece and finally
in Rome, Paul is forced to turn from the Jews to the
gentiles. Yet each time he has already converted a
number of Jews, and turns away from them with a
biblical gesture of abandonment (13:43,51; 18:6-8; 28:24-
28). On the third occasion, in the final verses of the book,
he quotes Isaiah to attest that this was predestined by
God.

Throughout the book Luke is careful to show that the
Roman authorities, who dominated the mediterranean

world at this time, are sympathetic towards Christianity and find no fault with its adherents. A Roman centurion is the first gentile to be converted (Ch.10). Paul himself is presented as a Roman citizen; as soon as Paul begins his mission the proconsul of Cyprus becomes a believer (13:12); the Roman governor of Achaia throws out Jewish accusations against Paul (18:12-17); in the final chapters the Roman authorities positively protect Paul against Jewish riots and plots, grant him a sympathetic hearing, and declare him innocent (25:25). It has often been suggested that Luke labours this point in order to gain favour for Christianity among the Roman authorities and show them that they have nothing to fear from it. More recently it has been suggested that Luke's direction of interest is the opposite: writing for a Christian rather than a Roman audience, he is concerned to show Christians that they have nothing to fear from the Roman authorities. Once the message has reached the hub of the empire, there is nothing to stop it, guided and directed by the Holy Spirit, from continuing its spread through the whole world.

☙ THE ACTS OF THE APOSTLES ☙

1 ¹In my earlier work,[a] Theophilus, I dealt with everything Jesus had done and taught from the beginning ²until the day he gave his instructions to the apostles he had chosen through the Holy Spirit, and was taken up to heaven. ³He had shown himself alive to them after his Passion by many demonstrations: for forty days he had continued to appear to them and tell them about the kingdom of God. ⁴When he had been at table with them, he had told them not to leave Jerusalem, but to wait there for what the Father had promised. 'It is' he had said 'what you have heard me speak about: ⁵John baptised with water but you, not many days from now, will be baptised with the Holy Spirit.'

The ascension

⁶Now having met together,[b] they asked him, 'Lord, has the time come? Are you going to restore the kingdom to Israel?' ⁷He replied, 'It is not for you to know times or dates that the Father has decided by his own authority, ⁸but you will receive power when the Holy Spirit comes on you, and then you will be my witnesses not only in Jerusalem but throughout Judaea and Samaria, and indeed to the ends of the earth'. ⁹As he said this he was lifted up while they looked on, and a cloud took him from their

---

[1a.] The gospel according to Luke.

[1b.] This verse takes up the narrative broken off in Lk 24:49.

sight. [10]They were still staring into the sky when suddenly two men in white were standing near them [11]and they said, 'Why are you men from Galilee standing here looking into the sky? Jesus who has been taken up from you into heaven, this same Jesus will come back in the same way as you have seen him go there.'

I. THE JERUSALEM CHURCH

The group of apostles

[12]So from the Mount of Olives, as it is called, they went back to Jerusalem, a short distance away, no more than a sabbath walk; [13]and when they reached the city they went to the upper room where they were staying; there were Peter and John, James and Andrew, Philip and Thomas, Bartholomew and Matthew, James son of Alphaeus and Simon the Zealot, and Jude son of James.[c] [14]All these joined in continuous prayer, together with several women, including Mary the mother of Jesus, and with his brothers.[d]

The election of Matthias

[15]One day Peter stood up to speak to the brothers[e] - there were about a hundred and twenty persons in the

---

[c] 'Son' (of Alphaeus, of James) is not in the Greek. This Jude is not the Jude 'brother' of Jesus, Mt 13:55 and Mk 6:3, and brother of James (Jude 1). Nor is it likely that 'James of Alphaeus' was James brother of the Lord.
[d] Cousins, as in the gospels.
[e] The term for Christians, usually the laity as distinct from apostles and elders.

congregation: [16]'Brothers, the passage of scripture had to be fulfilled in which the Holy Spirit, speaking through David, foretells the fate of Judas, who offered himself as a guide to the men who arrested Jesus - [17]after having been one of our number and actually sharing this ministry of ours. [18]As you know, he bought a field with the money he was paid for his crime. He fell headlong and burst open, and all his entrails poured out. [19]Everybody in Jerusalem heard about it and the field came to be called the Bloody Acre, in their language Hakeldama. [20]Now in the Book of Psalms it says: "Let his camp be reduced to ruin, Let there be no one to live in it."[f] And again: "Let someone else take his office."[g] [21]We must therefore choose someone who has been with us the whole time that the Lord Jesus was travelling round with us, [22]someone who was with us right from the time when John was baptising until the day when he was taken up from us - and he can act with us as a witness to his resurrection.' [23]Having nominated two candidates, Joseph known as Barsabbas, whose surname was Justus, and Matthias, [24]they prayed, 'Lord, you can read everyone's heart; show us therefore which of these two you have chosen [25]to take over this ministry and apostolate, which Judas abandoned to go to his proper place'. [26]They then drew lots for them, and as the lot fell to Matthias, he was listed as one of the twelve apostles.

[1f.] Ps 69:25
[1g.] Ps 109:8

ACTS 2:13

Pentecost

2 ¹When Pentecost day came round, they had all met in one room, ²when suddenly they heard what sounded like a powerful wind from heaven, the noise of which filled the entire house in which they were sitting; ³and something appeared to them that seemed like tongues of fire; these separated and came to rest on the head of each of them. ⁴They were all filled with the Holy Spirit, and began to speak foreign languages as the Spirit gave them the gift of speech. ⁵Now there were devout men living in Jerusalem from every nation under heaven, ⁶and at this sound they all assembled, each one bewildered to hear these men speaking his own language. ⁷They were amazed and astonished. 'Surely' they said 'all these men speaking are Galileans? ⁸How does it happen that each of us hears them in his own native language? ⁹Parthians, Medes and Elamites; people from Mesopotamia, Judaea and Cappadocia, Pontus and Asia, ¹⁰Phrygia and Pamphylia, Egypt and the parts of Libya round Cyrene; as well as visitors from Rome - ¹¹Jews and proselytes[a] alike - Cretans and Arabs; we hear them preaching in our own language about the marvels of God.' ¹²Everyone was amazed and unable to explain it; they asked one another what it all meant. ¹³Some, however, laughed it off. 'They have been drinking too much new wine' they said.

[2a] Converts from paganism.

Peter's address to the crowd

[14]Then Peter stood up with the Eleven and addressed them in a loud voice: 'Men of Judaea, and all you who live in Jerusalem, make no mistake about this, but listen carefully to what I say. [15]These men are not drunk, as you imagine; why, it is only the third hour of the day.[b] [16]On the contrary, this is what the prophet[c] spoke of: [17]"In the days to come - it is the Lord who speaks - I will pour out my spirit on all mankind. Their sons and daughters shall prophesy, your young men shall see visions, your old men shall dream dreams. [18]Even on my slaves, men and women, in those days, I will pour out my spirit. [19]I will display portents in heaven above and signs on earth below. [20]The sun will be turned into darkness and the moon into blood before the great Day of the Lord dawns. [21]All who call on the name of the Lord will be saved." [22]Men of Israel, listen to what I am going to say: Jesus the Nazarene was a man commended to you by God by the miracles and portents and signs that God worked through him when he was among you, as you all know. [23]This man, who was put into your power by the deliberate intention and foreknowledge of God, you took and had crucified by men outside the Law.[d] You killed him, [24]but God raised him to life, freeing him from the pangs of Hades; for it was impossible for him to be held in

---

[2b.] About 9 am
[2c.] Joel. See Jl 3:1-5.
[2d.] The Romans.

its power since, [25]as David says of him: "I saw the Lord before me always, for with him at my right hand nothing can shake me. [26]So my heart was glad and my tongue cried out with joy; my body, too, will rest in the hope [27]that you will not abandon my soul to Hades nor allow your holy one to experience corruption. [28]You have made known the way of life to me, you will fill me with gladness through your presence."[e] [29]Brothers, no one can deny that the patriarch David himself is dead and buried: his tomb is still with us. [30]But since he was a prophet, and knew that God had sworn him an oath to make one of his descendants succeed him on the throne,[f] [31]what he foresaw and spoke about was the resurrection of the Christ: he is the one who was not abandoned to Hades, and whose body did not experience corruption. [32]God raised this man Jesus to life, and all of us are witnesses to that. [33]Now raised to the heights by God's right hand, he has received from the Father the Holy Spirit, who was promised, and what you see and hear is the outpouring of that Spirit. [34]For David himself never went up to heaven; and yet these words are his: "The Lord said to my Lord: Sit at my right hand [35]until I make your enemies a footstool for you."[g] [36]For this reason the whole House of Israel can be certain that God has made this Jesus whom you crucified both Lord and Christ.'

[2e] Ps 16:8-11; quoted according to the LXX.

[2f] 2 S 7:12 and Ps 132:11

[2g] Ps 110:1

15

The first conversions

[37]Hearing this, they were cut to the heart and said to Peter and the apostles, 'What must we do, brothers?' [38]'You must repent,' Peter answered 'and every one of you must be baptised in the name of Jesus Christ for the forgiveness of your sins, and you will receive the gift of the Holy Spirit. [39]The promise that was made is for you and your children, and for all those who are far away, for all those whom the Lord our God will call to himself.'[h] [40]He spoke to them for a long time using many arguments, and he urged them, 'Save yourselves from this perverse generation'. [41]They were convinced by his arguments, and they accepted what he said and were baptised. That very day about three thousand were added to their number.

The early Christian community

[42]These remained faithful to the teaching of the apostles, to the brotherhood, to the breaking of bread and to the prayers. [43]The many miracles and signs worked through the apostles made a deep impression on everyone. [44]The faithful all lived together and owned everything in common; [45]they sold their goods and possessions and shared out the proceeds among themselves according to what each one needed. [46]They went as a body to the Temple every day but met in their houses for the breaking of bread; they shared their food gladly and generously;

[2 h.] Is 57:19

[47]they praised God and were looked up to by everyone. Day by day the Lord added to their community those destined to be saved.

The cure of a lame man

3 [1]Once, when Peter and John were going up to the Temple for the prayers at the ninth hour,[a] [2]it happened that there was a man being carried past. He was a cripple from birth; and they used to put him down every day near the Temple entrance called the Beautiful Gate so that he could beg from the people going in. [3]When this man saw Peter and John on their way into the Temple he begged from them. [4]Both Peter and John looked straight at him and said, 'Look at us'. [5]He turned to them expectantly, hoping to get something from them, [6]but Peter said, 'I have neither silver nor gold, but I will give you what I have: in the name of Jesus Christ the Nazarene, walk!' [7]Peter then took him by the hand and helped him to stand up. Instantly his feet and ankles became firm, [8]he jumped up, stood, and began to walk, and he went with them into the Temple, walking and jumping and praising God. [9]Everyone could see him walking and praising God, [10]and they recognised him as the man who used to sit begging at the Beautiful Gate of the Temple. They were all astonished and unable to explain what had happened to him.

[3a]. The time of evening sacrifice.

Peter's address to the people

[11]Everyone came running towards them in great excitement, to the Portico of Solomon, as it is called, where the man was still clinging to Peter and John. [12]When Peter saw the people he addressed them, 'Why are you so surprised at this? Why are you staring at us as though we had made this man walk by our own power or holiness? [13]You are Israelites, and it is the God of Abraham, Isaac and Jacob, the God of our ancestors, who has glorified his servant[b] Jesus, the same Jesus you handed over and then disowned in the presence of Pilate after Pilate had decided to release him. [14]It was you who accused the Holy One, the Just One, you who demanded the reprieve of a murderer [15]while you killed the prince of life. God, however, raised him from the dead, and to that fact we are the witnesses; [16]and it is the name of Jesus which, through our faith in it, has brought back the strength of this man whom you see here and who is well known to you. It is faith in that name that has restored this man to health, as you can all see. [17]Now I know, brothers, that neither you nor your leaders had any idea what you were really doing; [18]this was the way God carried out what he had foretold, when he said through all his prophets that his Christ would suffer. [19]Now you must repent and turn to God, so that your sins may be wiped out, [20]and so that the Lord may send the time of comfort. Then

---

[3 b.] Ex 3:6, 15 and Is 52:13

he will send you the Christ he has predestined, that is Jesus, [21]whom heaven must keep till the universal restoration comes which God proclaimed, speaking through his holy prophets. [22]Moses, for example, said: "The Lord God will raise up a prophet like myself for you, from among your own brothers; you must listen to whatever he tells you. [23]The man who does not listen to that prophet is to be cut off from the people."[c] [24]In fact, all the prophets that have ever spoken, from Samuel onwards, have predicted these days. [25]You are the heirs of the prophets, the heirs of the covenant God made with our ancestors when he told Abraham: in your offspring all the families of the earth will be blessed.[d] [26]It was for you in the first place that God raised up his servant and sent him to bless you by turning every one of you from your wicked ways.'

Peter and John before the Sanhedrin

4 [1]While they were still talking to the people the priests came up to them, accompanied by the captain of the Temple and the Sadducees.[a] [2]They were extremely annoyed at their teaching the people the doctrine of the resurrection from the dead by proclaiming the resurrection of Jesus. [3]They arrested them, but as it was already late, they held them till the next day. [4]But many of those who had listened

[3c.] Dt 18:18, 19

[3d.] Gn 12:3

[4a.] The Sadducees are always represented as denying the doctrine of the resurrection, e.g. Ac 23.

to their message became believers, the total number of whom had now risen to something like five thousand. ⁵The next day the rulers, elders and scribes^b had a meeting in Jerusalem ⁶with Annas the high priest, Caiaphas, Jonathan, Alexander and all the members of the high-priestly families. ⁷They made the prisoners stand in the middle and began to interrogate them, 'By what power, and by whose name have you men done this?' ⁸Then Peter, filled with the Holy Spirit, addressed them, 'Rulers of the people, and elders! ⁹If you are questioning us today about an act of kindness to a cripple, and asking us how he was healed, ¹⁰then I am glad to tell you all, and would indeed be glad to tell the whole people of Israel, that it was by the name of Jesus Christ the Nazarene, the one you crucified, whom God raised from the dead, by this name and by no other that this man is able to stand up perfectly healthy, here in your presence, today. ¹¹This is the stone rejected by you the builders, but which has proved to be the keystone.^c ¹²For of all the names in the world given to men, this is the only one by which we can be saved.' ¹³They were astonished at the assurance shown by Peter and John, considering they were uneducated laymen; and they recognised them as associates of Jesus; ¹⁴but when they saw the man who had been cured standing by their side, they could find no answer. ¹⁵So they ordered them to stand outside while the Sanhedrin had a private discussion.

---

^{4 b.} I.e. the Sanhedrin, explained for the non-Jewish reader.
^{4 c.} Ps 118:22

[16]'What are we going to do with these men?' they asked. 'It is obvious to everybody in Jerusalem that a miracle has been worked through them in public, and we cannot deny it. [17]But to stop the whole thing spreading any further among the people, let us caution them never to speak to anyone in this name again.' [18]So they called them in and gave them a warning on no account to make statements or to teach in the name of Jesus. [19]But Peter and John retorted, 'You must judge whether in God's eyes it is right to listen to you and not to God. [20]We cannot promise to stop proclaiming what we have seen and heard.' [21]The court repeated the warnings and then released them; they could not think of any way to punish them, since all the people were giving glory to God for what had happened. [22]The man who had been miraculously cured was over forty years old.

The apostles' prayer under persecution

[23]As soon as they were released they went to the community and told them everything the chief priests and elders had said to them. [24]When they heard it they lifted up their voice to God all together. 'Master,' they prayed 'it is you who made heaven and earth and sea, and everything in them; [25]you it is who said through the Holy Spirit and speaking through our ancestor David, your servant: "Why this arrogance among the nations, these futile plots among the peoples? [26]Kings on earth setting out to war, princes making an alliance, against

the Lord and against his Anointed."[d] [27]This is what has come true: in this very city Herod and Pontius Pilate made an alliance with the pagan nations and the peoples of Israel, against your holy servant Jesus whom you anointed,[e] [28]but only to bring about the very thing that you in your strength and your wisdom had predetermined should happen. [29]And now, Lord, take note of their threats and help your servants to proclaim your message with all boldness, [30]by stretching out your hand to heal and to work miracles and marvels through the name of your holy servant Jesus.' [31]As they prayed, the house where they were assembled rocked; they were all filled with the Holy Spirit and began to proclaim the word of God boldly.

The early Christian community

[32]The whole group of believers was united, heart and soul; no one claimed for his own use anything that he had, as everything they owned was held in common. [33]The apostles continued to testify to the resurrection of the Lord Jesus with great power, and they were all given great respect. [34]None of their members was ever in want, as all those who owned land or houses would sell them, and bring the money from them, [35]to present it to the apostles; it was then distributed to any members who might be in need.

---

4 d. Ps 2:1-2

4 e. I.e. made the Christ, the anointed Messiah.

The generosity of Barnabas

³⁶There was a Levite of Cypriot origin called Joseph whom the apostles surnamed Barnabas (which means 'son of encouragement'). ³⁷He owned a piece of land and he sold it and brought the money, and presented it to the apostles.

The fraud of Ananias and Sapphira

5 ¹There was another man, however, called Ananias. He and his wife, Sapphira, agreed to sell a property; ²but with his wife's connivance he kept back part of the proceeds, and brought the rest and presented it to the apostles. ³'Ananias,' Peter said 'how can Satan have so possessed you that you should lie to the Holy Spirit and keep back part of the money from the land? ⁴While you still owned the land, wasn't it yours to keep, and after you had sold it wasn't the money yours to do with as you liked? What put this scheme into your mind? It is not to men that you have lied, but to God.' ⁵When he heard this Ananias fell down dead. This made a profound impression on everyone present. ⁶The younger men got up, wrapped the body in a sheet, carried it out and buried it. ⁷About three hours later his wife came in, not knowing what had taken place. ⁸Peter challenged her, 'Tell me, was this the price you sold the land for?' 'Yes,' she said 'that was the price.' ⁹Peter then said, 'So you and your husband have agreed to put the Spirit of the Lord to the test! What made you do it? You hear those footsteps?

They have just been to bury your husband; they will carry you out, too.' [10]Instantly she dropped dead at his feet. When the young men came in they found she was dead, and they carried her out and buried her by the side of her husband. [11]This made a profound impression on the whole Church and on all who heard it.

The general situation

[12b]They all used to meet by common consent in the Portico of Solomon. [13]No one else ever dared to join them, but the people were loud in their praise [14]and the numbers of men and women who came to believe in the Lord increased steadily. [12a]So many signs and wonders were worked among the people at the hands of the apostles [15]that the sick were even taken out into the streets and laid on beds and sleeping-mats in the hope that at least the shadow of Peter might fall across some of them as he went past. [16]People even came crowding in from the towns round about Jerusalem, bringing with them their sick and those tormented by unclean spirits, and all of them were cured.

The apostles' arrest and miraculous deliverance

[17]Then the high priest intervened with all his supporters from the party of the Sadducees. Prompted by jealousy, [18]they arrested the apostles and had them put in the common gaol. [19]But at night the angel of the Lord opened the prison gates and said as he led them out, [20]'Go and stand in the Temple, and tell the people all about this new

Life'. ²¹They did as they were told; they went into the Temple at dawn and began to preach.

A summons to appear before the Sanhedrin

When the high priest arrived, he and his supporters convened the Sanhedrin - this was the full Senate of Israel - and sent to the gaol for them to be brought. ²²But when the officials arrived at the prison they found they were not inside, so they went back and reported, ²³'We found the gaol securely locked and the warders on duty at the gates, but when we unlocked the door we found no one inside'. ²⁴When the captain of the Temple and the chief priests heard this news they wondered what this could mean. ²⁵Then a man arrived with fresh news. 'At this very moment' he said 'the men you imprisoned are in the Temple. They are standing there preaching to the people.' ²⁶The captain went with his men and fetched them. They were afraid to use force in case the people stoned them. ²⁷When they had brought them in to face the Sanhedrin, the high priest demanded an explanation. ²⁸'We gave you a formal warning' he said 'not to preach in this name, and what have you done? You have filled Jerusalem with your teaching, and seem determined to fix the guilt of this man's death on us.' ²⁹In reply Peter and the apostles said, 'Obedience to God comes before obedience to men; ³⁰it was the God of our ancestors who raised up Jesus, but it was you who had him executed by hanging on a tree.[a] [31]By his own right hand God has now raised him up to be leader and saviour, to give repentance and forgiveness of sins through him to Israel. [32]We are witnesses to all this, we and the Holy Spirit whom God has given to those who obey him.' [33]This so infuriated them that they wanted to put them to death.

Gamaliel's intervention

[34]One member of the Sanhedrin, however, a Pharisee called Gamaliel, who was a doctor of the Law and respected by the whole people,[b] stood up and asked to have the men taken outside for a time. [35]Then he addressed the Sanhedrin, 'Men of Israel, be careful how you deal with these people. [36]There was Theudas who became notorious not so long ago. He claimed to be someone important, and he even collected about four hundred followers; but when he was killed, all his followers scattered and that was the end of them. [37]And then there was Judas the Galilean, at the time of the census, who attracted crowds of supporters; but he got killed too, and all his followers dispersed. [38]What I suggest, therefore, is that you leave these men alone and let them go. If this enterprise, this movement of theirs, is of human origin it will break up of its own accord; [39]but if it does in fact come from God you will not only be unable to destroy

---

5 a. the phrase recalls Dt 21:23.
5 b. Gamaliel I, a Pharisee of the school of Hillel; he was Paul's teacher.

them, but you might find yourselves fighting against God.' His advice was accepted; [40]and they had the apostles called in, gave orders for them to be flogged, warned them not to speak in the name of Jesus and released them. [41]And so they left the presence of the Sanhedrin glad to have had the honour of suffering humiliation for the sake of the name. [42]They preached every day both in the Temple and in private houses, and their proclamation of the Good News of Christ Jesus was never interrupted.

II. THE EARLIEST MISSIONS

The institution of the Seven

6 [1]About this time, when the number of disciples was increasing, the Hellenists made a complaint against the Hebrews:[a] in the daily distribution their own widows were being overlooked. [2]So the Twelve called a full meeting of the disciples and addressed them, 'It would not be right for us to neglect the word of God so as to give out food; [3]you, brothers, must select from among yourselves seven men of good reputation, filled with the Spirit and with wisdom; we will hand over this duty to them, [4]and continue to devote ourselves to prayer and to the service of the word'. [5]The whole assembly approved

---

[6a] 'Hellenists': Jews from outside Palestine; they had their own synagogues in Jerusalem, where the scriptures were read in Greek. The 'Hebrews' were Palestinian Jews and in their synagogues scriptures were read in Hebrew.

of this proposal and elected Stephen, a man full of faith and of the Holy Spirit, together with Philip, Prochorus, Nicanor, Timon, Parmenas, and Nicolaus of Antioch, a convert to Judaism. ⁶They presented these to the apostles, who prayed and laid their hands on them.ᵇ ⁷The word of the Lord continued to spread: the number of disciples in Jerusalem was greatly increased, and a large group of priests made their submission to the faith.

Stephen's arrest

⁸Stephen was filled with grace and power and began to work miracles and great signs among the people. ⁹But then certain people came forward to debate with Stephen, some from Cyrene and Alexandria who were members of the synagogue called the Synagogue of Freedmen,ᶜ and others from Cilicia and Asia. ¹⁰They found they could not get the better of him because of his wisdom, and because it was the Spirit that prompted what he said. ¹¹So they procured some men to say, 'We heard him using blasphemous language against Moses and against God'. ¹²Having in this way turned the people against him as well as the elders and scribes, they took Stephen by surprise, and arrested him and brought him before the Sanhedrin. ¹³There they put up false witnesses to say, 'This man is always making speeches against this Holy

---

⁶ᵇ. 'and they prayed and laid their hands on them'; probably meaning the apostles, handing over their duties as in v.3.
⁶ᶜ. Probably the descendants of Jews carried off to Rome, 63 BC and sold as slaves but later released.

Place and the Law. [14]We have heard him say that Jesus the Nazarene is going to destroy this Place and alter the traditions that Moses handed down to us.' [15]The members of the Sanhedrin all looked intently at Stephen, and his face appeared to them like the face of an angel.

Stephen's speech

7 [1]The high priest asked, 'Is this true?' [2]He replied, 'My brothers, my fathers, listen to what I have to say. The God of glory appeared to our ancestor Abraham, while he was in Mesopotamia before settling in Haran, [3]and said to him, "Leave your country and your family and go to the land I will show you".[a] [4]So he left Chaldaea and settled in Haran; and after his father died God made him leave Haran and come to this land where you are living today. [5]God did not give him a single square foot of this land to call his own, yet he promised to give it to him and after him to his descendants, childless[b] though he was. [6]The actual words God used when he spoke to him are that his descendants would be exiles in a foreign land, where they would be slaves and oppressed for four hundred years. [7]"But I will pass judgement on the nation that enslaves them" God said "and after this they will leave, and worship me in this place."[c] [8]Then he made the covenant of circumcision: so

---

[7a] Gn 12:1
[7b] Gn 15:2
[7c] Gn 15:2, 13, 14; Ex 3:12

when his son Isaac was born he circumcised him on the eighth day. Isaac did the same for Jacob, and Jacob for the twelve patriarchs. ⁹The patriarchs were jealous of Joseph and sold him into slavery in Egypt.ᵈ But God was with him,ᵉ ¹⁰and rescued him from all his miseries by making him wise enough to attract the attention of Pharoah king of Egypt, who made him governor of Egyptᶠ and put him in charge of the royal household. ¹¹Then a famine came that caused much suffering throughout Egypt and Canaan, and our ancestors could find nothing to eat. ¹²When Jacob heard that there was grain for sale in Egypt, he sent our ancestors there on a first visit, ¹³but it was on the second that Joseph made himself known to his brothers, and told Pharaoh about his family. ¹⁴Joseph then sent for his father Jacob and his whole family, a total of seventy-five people. ¹⁵Jacob went down into Egypt and after he and our ancestors had died there, ¹⁶their bodies were brought back to Shechem and buried in the tomb that Abraham had bought and paid for from the sons of Hamor, the father of Shechem. ¹⁷As the time drew near for God to fulfil the promise he had solemnly made to Abraham, our nation in Egypt grew larger and larger, ¹⁸until a new king came to power in Egypt who knew nothing ofᵍ

---

7 d. Gn 37

7 e. Gn 39

7 f. Gn 41. Other direct quotations and allusions in this paragraph are from Gn 42-50.

7 g. OT quotations from here to v.35 are from Ex 1-3.

Joseph. [19]He exploited our race, and ill-treated our ancestors, forcing them to expose their babies to prevent their surviving. [20]It was at this period that Moses was born, a fine child and favoured by God. He was looked after for three months in his father's house, [21]and after he had been exposed, Pharaoh's daughter adopted him and brought him up as her own son. [22]So Moses was taught all the wisdom of the Egyptians and became a man with power both in his speech and his actions. [23]At the age of forty he decided to visit his countrymen, the sons of Israel. [24]When he saw one of them being ill-treated he went to his defence and rescued the man by killing the Egyptian. [25]He thought his brothers realised that through him God would liberate them, but they did not. [26]The next day, when he came across some of them fighting, he tried to reconcile them. "Friends," he said "you are brothers; why are you hurting each other?" [27]But the man who was attacking his fellow countryman pushed him aside. "And who appointed you" he said "to be our leader and judge? [28]Do you intend to kill me as you killed the Egyptian yesterday?" [29]Moses fled when he heard this[h] and he went to stay in the land of Midian, where he became the father of two sons. [30]Forty years later, in the wilderness near Mount Sinai, an angel appeared to him in the flames of a bush that was on fire. [31]Moses was amazed by what he saw. As he went nearer to look at it the voice of the Lord was

---

[7h]. In Ex 2:15 Moses runs away because he is afraid of Pharaoh.

heard, [32]"I am the God of your ancestors, the God of Abraham, Isaac and Jacob". Moses trembled and did not dare to look any more. [33]The Lord said to him, "Take off your shoes; the place where you are standing is holy ground. [34]I have seen the way my people are ill-treated in Egypt, I have heard their groans, and I have come down to liberate them. So come here and let me send you into Egypt." [35]It was the same Moses that they had disowned when they said, "Who appointed you to be our leader and judge?" who was now sent to be both leader and redeemer through the angel who had appeared to him in the bush. [36]It was Moses who, after performing miracles and signs in Egypt, led them out across the Red Sea and through the wilderness for forty years.[i] [37]It was Moses who told the sons of Israel, "God will raise up a prophet like myself for you from among your own brothers".[j] [38]When they held the assembly in the wilderness it was only through Moses that our ancestors could communicate with the angel who had spoken to him on Mount Sinai; it was he who was entrusted with words of life to hand on to us. [39]This is the man that our ancestors refused to listen to: they pushed him aside, turned back to Egypt in their thoughts, [40]and said to Aaron, "Make some gods to be our leaders; we do not understand what has come over this Moses who led us out of Egypt".[k]

[7i.] Nb 14:33
[7j.] Dt 18:15, 18
[7k.] Ex 32:1, 23 and 32:4, 6

[41]It was then that they made a bull calf and offered sacrifice to the idol. They were perfectly happy with something they had made for themselves. [42]God turned away from them and abandoned them to the worship of the army of heaven,[l] as scripture says in the book of the prophets: "Did you bring me victims and sacrifices in the wilderness for all those forty years, you House of Israel? [43]No, you carried the tent of Moloch on your shoulders and the star of the god Rephan, those idols that you had made to adore. So now I will exile you even further than Babylon."[m] [44]While they were in the desert our ancestors possessed the Tent of Testimony that had been constructed according to the instructions God gave Moses, telling him to make an exact copy of the pattern[n] he had been shown. [45]It was handed down from one ancestor of ours to another until Joshua brought it into the country we had conquered from the nations which were driven out by God as we advanced. Here it stayed until the time of David. [46]He won God's favour and asked permission to have a temple built for the House of Jacob, [47]though it was Solomon who actually built God's house[o] for him. [48]Even so the Most High does not live in a house that human hands have built: for as the prophet says: [49]"With heaven my throne and earth my footstool,

---

[l] The stars and planets.

[m] Am 5:25-27 (LXX)

[n] Ex 25:40

[o] 1 K 6:2

33

what house could you build me, what place could you make for my rest? [50]Was not all this made by my hand?"[p] [51]You stubborn people, with your pagan hearts and pagan ears. You are always resisting the Holy Spirit, just as your ancestors used to do. [52]Can you name a single prophet your ancestors never persecuted? In the past they killed those who foretold the coming of the Just One, and now you have become his betrayers, his murderers. [53]You who had the Law brought to you by angels are the very ones who have not kept it.' [54]They were infuriated when they heard this, and ground their teeth at him.

The stoning of Stephen. Saul as persecutor

[55]But Stephen, filled with the Holy Spirit, gazed into heaven and saw the glory of God, and Jesus standing at God's right hand. [56]'I can see heaven thrown open' he said 'and the Son of Man standing at the right hand of God.' [57]At this all the members of the council shouted out and stopped their ears with their hands; then they all rushed at him, [58]sent him out of the city and stoned him. The witnesses[q] put down their clothes at the feet of a young man called Saul. [59]As they were stoning him, Stephen said in invocation, 'Lord Jesus, receive my spirit'. [60]Then he knelt down and said aloud, 'Lord, do not hold this sin against them'; and with these words he fell asleep.

[7p.] Is 66:1-2

[7q.] By the Law, the accusers had to begin the execution of the sentence.

8 ¹Saul entirely approved of the killing. That day a bitter persecution started against the church in Jerusalem, and everyoneᵃ except the apostles fled to the country districts of Judaea and Samaria. ²There were some devout people, however, who buried Stephen and made great mourning for him. ³Saul then worked for the total destruction of the Church; he went from house to house arresting both men and women and sending them to prison.

Philip in Samaria

⁴Those who had escaped went from place to place preaching the Good News. ⁵One of them was Philip who went to a Samaritan town and proclaimed the Christ to them. ⁶The people united in welcoming the message Philip preached, either because they had heard of the miracles he worked or because they saw them for themselves. ⁷There were, for example, unclean spirits that came shrieking out of many who were possessed, and several paralytics and cripples were cured. ⁸As a result there was great rejoicing in that town.

Simon the magician

⁹Now a man called Simon had already practised magic arts in the town and astounded the Samaritan people. He had given it out that he was someone momentous, ¹⁰and everyone believed what he said; eminent citizens and

---

⁸ᵃ The persecution seems to have been directed principally against the Hellenists.

ordinary people alike had declared, 'He is the divine power that is called Great'. ¹¹They had only been won over to him because of the long time he had spent working on them with his magic. ¹²But when they believed Philip's preaching of the Good News about the kingdom of God and the name of Jesus Christ, they were baptised, both men and women, ¹³and even Simon himself became a believer. After his baptism Simon, who went round constantly with Philip, was astonished when he saw the wonders and great miracles that took place. ¹⁴When the apostles in Jerusalem heard that Samaria had accepted the word of God, they sent Peter and John to them, ¹⁵and they went down there, and prayed for the Samaritans to receive the Holy Spirit, ¹⁶for as yet he had not come down on any of them: they had only been baptised in the name of the Lord Jesus. ¹⁷Then they laid hands on them, and they received the Holy Spirit. ¹⁸When Simon saw that the Spirit was given through the imposition of hands by the apostles, he offered them some money. ¹⁹'Give me the same power' he said 'so that anyone I lay my hands on will receive the Holy Spirit.' ²⁰Peter answered, 'May your silver be lost forever, and you with it, for thinking that money could buy what God has given for nothing! ²¹You have no share, no rights, in this: God can see how your heart is warped. ²²Repent of this wickedness of yours, and pray to the Lord; you may still be forgiven for thinking as you did; ²³it is plain to me that you are trapped in the bitterness of gall and the chains of sin.' [24]'Pray to the Lord for me yourselves' Simon replied 'so that none of the things you have spoken about may happen to me.' [25]Having given their testimony and proclaimed the word of the Lord, they went back to Jerusalem, preaching the Good News to a number of Samaritan villages.

Philip baptises a eunuch

[26]The angel of the Lord spoke to Philip saying, 'Be ready to set out at noon along the road that goes from Jerusalem down to Gaza, the desert road'. [27]So he set off on his journey. Now it happened that an Ethiopian had been on pilgrimage to Jerusalem; he was a eunuch and an officer at the court of the kandake, or queen, of Ethiopia, and was in fact her chief treasurer. [28]He was now on his way home; and as he sat in his chariot he was reading the prophet Isaiah. [29]The Spirit said to Philip, 'Go up and meet that chariot'. [30]When Philip ran up, he heard him reading Isaiah the prophet and asked, 'Do you understand what you are reading?' [31]'How can I' he replied 'unless I have someone to guide me?' So he invited Philip to get in and sit by his side. [32]Now the passage of scripture he was reading was this: "Like a sheep that is led to the slaughter-house, like a lamb that is dumb in front of its shearers, like these he never opens his mouth. [33]He has been humiliated and has no one to defend him. Who will ever talk about his

ACTS 8:34

descendants, since his life on earth has been cut short!'ᵇ ³⁴The eunuch turned to Philip and said, 'Tell me, is the prophet referring to himself or someone else?' ³⁵Starting, therefore, with this text of scripture Philip proceeded to explain the Good News of Jesus to him. ³⁶Further along the road they came to some water, and the eunuch said, 'Look, there is some water here; is there anything to stop me being baptised?'ᶜ ³⁸He ordered the chariot to stop, then Philip and the eunuch both went down into the water and Philip baptised him. ³⁹But after they had come up out of the water again Philip was taken away by the Spirit of the Lord, and the eunuch never saw him again but went on his way rejoicing. ⁴⁰Philip found that he had reached Azotus and continued his journey proclaiming the Good News in every town as far as Caesarea.

The conversion of Saul

9 ¹Meanwhile Saul was still breathing threats to slaughter the Lord's disciples. He had gone to the high priest ²and asked for letters addressed to the synagogues in Damascus, that would authorise him to arrest and take to Jerusalem any followers of the Way, men or women, that he could find. ³Suddenly, while he was travelling to Damascus and just before he reached the city, there came a light from

---

ᵇ Is 53:7-8, quoted from the LXX version.
ᶜ At the time when verse numbers were introduced, there was a gloss, numbered v.37, at this point.

38

heaven all round him. ⁴He fell to the ground, and then he heard a voice saying, 'Saul, Saul, why are you persecuting me?' ⁵'Who are you, Lord?' he asked, and the voice answered, 'I am Jesus, and you are persecuting me. ⁶Get up now and go into the city, and you will be told what you have to do.' ⁷The men travelling with Saul stood there speechless, for though they heard the voice they could see no one. ⁸Saul got up from the ground, but even with his eyes wide open he could see nothing at all, and they had to lead him into Damascus by the hand. ⁹For three days he was without his sight, and took neither food nor drink. ¹⁰A disciple called Ananias who lived in Damascus had a vision in which he heard the Lord say to him, 'Ananias!' When he replied, 'Here I am, Lord', ¹¹the Lord said, 'You must go to Straight Street and ask at the house of Judas for someone called Saul, who comes from Tarsus. At this moment he is praying, ¹²having had a vision of a man called Ananias coming in and laying hands on him to give him back his sight.' ¹³When he heard that, Ananias said, 'Lord, several people have told me about this man and all the harm he has been doing to your saints in Jerusalem. ¹⁴He has only come here because he holds a warrant from the chief priests to arrest everybody who invokes your name.' ¹⁵The Lord replied, 'You must go all the same, because this man is my chosen instrument to bring my name before pagans and pagan kings and before the people of Israel; ¹⁶I myself will show him how much he himself must suffer for my name'. [17]Then Ananias went. He entered the house, and at once laid his hands on Saul and said, 'Brother Saul, I have been sent by the Lord Jesus who appeared to you on your way here so that you may recover your sight and be filled with the Holy Spirit'. [18]Immediately it was as though scales fell away from Saul's eyes and he could see again. So he was baptised there and then, [19]and after taking some food he regained his strength.

Saul's preaching at Damascus

After he had spent only a few days with the disciples in Damascus, [20]he began preaching in the synagogues, 'Jesus is the Son of God'. [21]All his hearers were amazed. 'Surely' they said 'this is the man who organised the attack in Jerusalem against the people who invoke this name, and who came here for the sole purpose of arresting them to have them tried by the chief priests?' [22]Saul's power increased steadily, and he was able to throw the Jewish colony at Damascus into complete confusion by the way be demonstrated that Jesus was the Christ. [23]Some time passed,[a] and the Jews worked out a plot to kill him, [24]but news of it reached Saul. To make sure of killing him they kept watch on the gates day and night, [25]but when it was dark the disciples took him and let him down from the top of the wall, lowering him in a basket.

[9a.] Three years, according to Ga 1:17-18.

Saul's visit to Jerusalem

²⁶When he got to Jerusalem he tried to join the disciples, but they were all afraid of him: they could not believe he was really a disciple. ²⁷Barnabas, however, took charge of him, introduced him to the apostles, and explained how the Lord had appeared to Saul and spoken to him on his journey, and how he had preached boldly at Damascus in the name of Jesus. ²⁸Saul now started to go round with them in Jerusalem, preaching fearlessly in the name of the Lord. ²⁹But after he had spoken to the Hellenists, and argued with them, they became determined to kill him. ³⁰When the brothers knew, they took him to Caesarea, and sent him off from there to Tarsus.

A lull

³¹The churches throughout Judaea, Galilee and Samaria were now left in peace, building themselves up, living in the fear of the Lord, and filled with the consolation of the Holy Spirit.

Peter cures a paralytic at Lydda

³²Peter visited one place after another and eventually came to the saints living down in Lydda. ³³There he found a man called Aeneas, a paralytic who had been bedridden for eight years. ³⁴Peter said to him, 'Aeneas, Jesus Christ cures you: get up and fold up your sleeping mat'. Aeneas got up immediately; ³⁵everybody who lived in Lydda and Sharon saw him, and they were all converted to the Lord.

Peter raises a woman to life at Jaffa

[36]At Jaffa there was a woman disciple called Tabitha, or Dorcas in Greek,[b] who never tired of doing good or giving in charity. [37]But the time came when she got ill and died, and they washed her and laid her out in a room upstairs. [38]Lydda is not far from Jaffa, so when the disciples heard that Peter was there, they sent two men with an urgent message for him, 'Come and visit us as soon as possible'. [39]Peter went back with them straightaway, and on his arrival they took him to the upstairs room, where all the widows stood round him in tears, showing him tunics and other clothes Dorcas had made when she was with them. [40]Peter sent them all out of the room and knelt down and prayed. Then he turned to the dead woman and said, 'Tabitha, stand up'. She opened her eyes, looked at Peter and sat up. [41]Peter helped her to her feet, then he called in the saints and widows and showed them she was alive. [42]The whole of Jaffa heard about it and many believed in the Lord. [43]Peter stayed on some time in Jaffa, lodging with a leather-tanner called Simon.

Peter visits a Roman centurion

10 [1]One of the centurions of the Italica cohort stationed in Caesarea was called Cornelius. [2]He and the whole of his household were devout and God-fearing, and he gave generously to Jewish causes and prayed constantly to

9 b. I.e. 'Gazelle'.

God. ³One day at about the ninth hour he had a vision in which he distinctly saw the angel of God come into his house and call out to him, 'Cornelius!' ⁴He stared at the vision in terror and exclaimed, 'What is it, Lord?' 'Your offering of prayers and alms' the angel answered 'has been accepted by God. ⁵Now you must send someone to Jaffa and fetch a man called Simon, known as Peter, ⁶who is lodging with Simon the tanner whose house is by the sea.' ⁷When the angel who said this had gone, Cornelius called two of the slaves and a devout soldier of his staff, ⁸told them what had happened, and sent them off to Jaffa. ⁹Next day, while they were still on their journey and had only a short distance to go before reaching Jaffa, Peter went to the housetop at about the sixth hour to pray. ¹⁰He felt hungry and was looking forward to his meal, but before it was ready he fell into a trance ¹¹and saw heaven thrown open and something like a big sheet being let down to earth by its four corners; ¹²it contained every possible sort of animal and bird, walking, crawling or flying ones. ¹³A voice then said to him, 'Now, Peter; kill and eat!' ¹⁴But Peter answered, 'Certainly not, Lord; I have never yet eaten anything profane or unclean'. ¹⁵Again, a second time, the voice spoke to him, 'What God has made clean, you have no right to call profane'. ¹⁶This was repeated three times, and then suddenly the container was drawn up to heaven again. ¹⁷Peter was still worrying over the meaning of the vision he had seen, when the men sent by Cornelius arrived. They had asked where Simon's house was and they were now standing at the door, [18]calling out to know if the Simon known as Peter was lodging there. [19]Peter's mind was still on the vision and the Spirit had to tell him, 'Some men have come to see you. [20]Hurry down, and do not hesitate about going back with them; it was I who told them to come.' [21]Peter went down and said to them, 'I am the man you are looking for; why have you come?' [22]They said, 'The centurion Cornelius, who is an upright and God-fearing man, highly regarded by the entire Jewish people, was directed by a holy angel to send for you and bring you to his house and to listen to what you have to say'. [23]So Peter asked them in and gave them lodging. Next day, he was ready to go off with them, accompanied by some of the brothers from Jaffa. [24]They reached Caesarea the following day, and Cornelius was waiting for them. He had asked his relations and close friends to be there, [25]and as Peter reached the house Cornelius went out to meet him, knelt at his feet and prostrated himself. [26]But Peter helped him up. 'Stand up,' he said 'I am only a man after all!' [27]Talking together they went in to meet all the people assembled there, [28]and Peter said to them, 'You know it is forbidden for Jews to mix with people of another race and visit them, but God has made it clear to me that I must not call anyone profane or unclean. [29]That is why I made no objection to coming when I was sent for; but I should like to know exactly why you sent for me.' [30]Cornelius replied, 'Three days ago I was praying in my house at the ninth hour, when I suddenly saw a man in front of me in shining robes. [31]He said, "Cornelius, your prayer has been heard and your alms have been accepted as a sacrifice in the sight of God; [32]so now you must send to Jaffa and fetch Simon known as Peter who is lodging in the house of Simon the tanner, by the sea". [33]So I sent for you at once, and you have been kind enough to come. Here we all are, assembled in front of you to hear what message God has given you for us.'

Peter's address in the house of Cornelius

[34]Then Peter addressed them: 'The truth I have now come to realise' he said 'is that God does not have favourites, [35]but that anybody of any nationality who fears God and does what is right is acceptable to him. [36]It is true, God sent his word to the people of Israel, and it was to them that the good news of peace was brought[a] by Jesus Christ - but Jesus Christ is Lord of all men. [37]You must have heard about the recent happenings in Judaea; about Jesus of Nazareth and how he began in Galilee, after John had been preaching baptism. [38]God had anointed him with the Holy Spirit[b] and with power, and because God was with him, Jesus went about doing good and curing all who had fallen into the power of the

---

[10a.] Is 52:7
[10b.] Is 61:1

devil. [39]Now I, and those with me, can witness to everything he did throughout the countryside of Judaea and in Jerusalem itself: and also to the fact that they killed him by hanging him on a tree, [40]yet three days afterwards God raised him to life and allowed him to be seen, [41]not by the whole people but only by certain witnesses God had chosen beforehand. Now we are those witnesses - we have eaten and drunk with him after his resurrection from the dead - [42]and he has ordered us to proclaim this to his people and to tell them that God has appointed him to judge everyone, alive or dead. [43]It is to him that all the prophets bear this witness: that all who believe in Jesus will have their sins forgiven through his name.'

Baptism of the first pagans

[44]While Peter was still speaking the Holy Spirit came down on all the listeners. [45]Jewish believers who had accompanied Peter were astonished that the gift of the Holy Spirit should be poured out on the pagans too, [46]since they could hear them speaking strange languages and proclaiming the greatness of God. Peter himself then said, [47]'Could anyone refuse the water of baptism to these people, now they have received the Holy Spirit just as much as we have?' [48]He then gave orders for them to be baptised in the name of Jesus Christ. Afterwards they begged him to stay on for some days.

Jerusalem: Peter justifies his conduct

11 ¹The apostles and the brothers in Judaea heard that the pagans too had accepted the word of God, ²and when Peter came up to Jerusalem the Jews criticised him ³and said, 'So you have been visiting the uncircumcised and eating with them, have you?' ⁴Peter in reply gave them the details point by point: ⁵'One day, when I was in the town of Jaffa,' he began 'I fell into a trance as I was praying and had a vision of something like a big sheet being let down from heaven by its four corners. This sheet reached the ground quite close to me. ⁶I watched it intently and saw all sorts of animals and wild beasts - everything possible that could walk, crawl or fly. ⁷Then I heard a voice that said to me, "Now, Peter; kill and eat!" ⁸But I answered: Certainly not, Lord; nothing profane or unclean has ever crossed my lips. ⁹And a second time the voice spoke from heaven, "What God has made clean, you have no right to call profane". ¹⁰This was repeated three times, before the whole of it was drawn up to heaven again. ¹¹Just at that moment, three men stopped outside the house where we were staying; they had been sent from Caesarea to fetch me, ¹²and the Spirit told me to have no hesitation about going back with them. The six brothers here came with me as well, and we entered the man's house. ¹³He told us he had seen an angel standing in his house who said, "Send to Jaffa and fetch Simon known as Peter; ¹⁴he has a message for you that will save you and your entire

household". [15]I had scarcely begun to speak when the Holy Spirit came down on them in the same way as it came on us at the beginning, [16]and I remembered that the Lord had said, "John baptised with water, but you will be baptised with the Holy Spirit". [17]I realised then that God was giving them the identical thing he gave to us when we believed in the Lord Jesus Christ; and who was I to stand in God's way?' [18]This account satisfied them, and they gave glory to God. 'God' they said 'can evidently grant even the pagans the repentance that leads to life.'

Foundation of the church of Antioch

[19]Those who had escaped during the persecution that happened because of Stephen travelled as far as Phoenicia and Cyprus and Antioch,[a] but they usually proclaimed the message only to Jews. [20]Some of them, however, who came from Cyprus and Cyrene, went to Antioch where they started preaching to the Greeks, proclaiming the Good News of the Lord Jesus to them as well. [21]The Lord helped them, and a great number believed and were converted to the Lord. [22]The church in Jerusalem heard about this and they sent Barnabas to Antioch. [23]There he could see for himself that God had given grace, and this pleased him, and he urged them all to remain faithful to the Lord with heartfelt devotion; [24]for he was a good man, filled with the Holy Spirit and with

---

[11a.] Antioch on the Orontes, capital of Syria.

faith. And a large number of people were won over to the Lord. [25]Barnabas then left for Tarsus to look for Saul, [26]and when he found him he brought him to Antioch. As things turned out they were to live together in that church a whole year, instructing a large number of people. It was at Antioch that the disciples were first called 'Christians'.

Barnabas and Saul sent as deputies to Jerusalem

[27]While they were there some prophets[b] came down to Antioch from Jerusalem, [28]and one of them whose name was Agabus, seized by the Spirit, stood up and predicted that a famine would spread over the whole empire. This in fact happened before the reign of Claudius came to an end.[c] [29]The disciples decided to send relief, each to contribute what he could afford, to the brothers living in Judaea. [30]They did this and delivered their contributions to the elders in the care of Barnabas and Saul.

Peter's arrest and miraculous deliverance[a]

12 [1]It was about this time that King Herod started persecuting certain members of the Church. [2]He beheaded James the brother of John, [3]and when he saw that this pleased the Jews he decided to arrest Peter as

---

11 b. Christian prophets, inspired speakers, generally ranked second to the apostles in the lists of the persons 'gifted by the Spirit'.

11 c. Claudius reigned until 54 AD

12 a. Herod Agrippa I was king of Judaea and Samaria, 41-44 AD This episode, though fitted in the book between 11:30 and 12:25, must have taken place before Barnabas and Saul visited Jerusalem.

well. ⁴This was during the days of Unleavened Bread, and he put Peter in prison, assigning four squads of four soldiers each to guard him in turns. Herod meant to try Peter in public after the end of Passover week. ⁵All the time Peter was under guard the Church prayed to God for him unremittingly. ⁶On the night before Herod was to try him, Peter was sleeping between two soldiers, fastened with double chains, while guards kept watch at the main entrance to the prison. ⁷Then suddenly the angel of the Lord stood there, and the cell was filled with light. He tapped Peter on the side and woke him. 'Get up!' he said 'Hurry!' - and the chains fell from his hands. ⁸The angel then said, 'Put on your belt and sandals'. After he had done this, the angel next said, 'Wrap your cloak round you and follow me'. ⁹Peter followed him, but had no idea that what the angel did was all happening in reality; he thought he was seeing a vision. ¹⁰They passed through two guard posts one after the other, and reached the iron gate leading to the city. This opened of its own accord; they went through it and had walked the whole length of one street when suddenly the angel left him. ¹¹It was only then that Peter came to himself. 'Now I know it is all true' he said. The Lord really did send his angel and has saved me from Herod and from all that the Jewish people were so certain would happen to me.' ¹²As soon as he realised this he went straight to the house of Mary the mother of

John Mark,[b] where a number of people had assembled and were praying. [13]He knocked at the outside door and a servant called Rhoda came to answer it. [14]She recognised Peter's voice and was so overcome with joy that, instead of opening the door, she ran inside with the news that Peter was standing at the main entrance. [15]They said to her, 'You are out of your mind', but she insisted that it was true. Then they said, 'It must be his angel!' [16]Peter, meanwhile, was still knocking, so they opened the door and were amazed to see that it really was Peter himself. [17]With a gesture of his hand he stopped them talking, and described to them how the Lord had led him out of prison. He added, 'Tell James and the brothers'. Then he left and went to another place. [18]When daylight came there was a great commotion among the soldiers, who could not imagine what had become of Peter. [19]Herod put out an unsuccessful search for him; he had the guards questioned, and before leaving Judaea to take up residence in Caesarea he gave orders for their execution.

The death of the persecutor

[20]Now Herod was on bad terms with the Tyrians and Sidonians. However, they sent a joint deputation which managed to enlist the support of Blastus, the king's

---

12 b. Mark is mentioned in chapter 12, 13 and 15: also in Col 4 and Phm 24 and 2 Tim 4. Tradition names him as author of the second gospel.

chamberlain, and through him negotiated a treaty, since their country depended for its food supply on King Herod's territory. [21]A day was fixed, and Herod, wearing his robes of state and enthroned on a dais, made a speech to them. [22]The people acclaimed him with, 'It is a god speaking, not a man!', [23]and at that moment the angel of the Lord struck him down, because he had not given the glory to God. He was eaten away with worms and died.

Barnabas and Saul return to Antioch

[24]The word of God continued to spread and to gain followers. [25]Barnabas and Saul completed their task and came back from Jerusalem, bringing John Mark with them.

III. THE MISSION OF BARNABAS AND PAUL
THE COUNCIL OF JERUSALEM

The mission sent out

13 [1]In the church at Antioch the following were prophets and teachers: Barnabas, Simeon called Niger, and Lucius of Cyrene, Manaen, who had been brought up with Herod the tetrarch, and Saul. [2]One day while they were offering worship to the Lord and keeping a fast, the Holy Spirit said, 'I want Barnabas and Saul set apart for the work to which I have called them'. [3]So it was that after fasting and prayer they laid their hands on them and sent them off.

Cyprus: the magician Elymas

⁴So these two, sent on their mission by the Holy Spirit, went down to Seleucia and from there sailed to Cyprus. ⁵They landed at Salamis and proclaimed the word of God in the synagogues of the Jews; John acted as their assistant. ⁶They travelled the whole length of the island, and at Paphos they came in contact with a Jewish magician called Bar-jesus. ⁷This false prophet was one of the attendants of the proconsul Sergius Paulus who was an extremely intelligent man. The proconsul summoned Barnabas and Saul and asked to hear the word of God, ⁸but Elymas Magos - as he was called in Greek - tried to stop them so as to prevent the proconsul's conversion to the faith. ⁹Then Saul, whose other name is Paul, looked him full in the face ¹⁰and said, 'You utter fraud, you impostor, you son of the devil, you enemy of all true religion, why don't you stop twisting the straightforward ways of the Lord? ¹¹Now watch how the hand of the Lord will strike you: you will be blind, and for a time you will not see the sun.' That instant, everything went misty and dark for him, and he groped about to find someone to lead him by the hand. ¹²The proconsul, who had watched everything, became a believer, being astonished by what he had learnt about the Lord.

They arrive at Antioch in Pisidia

¹³Paul and his friends went by sea from Paphos to Perga in Pamphylia where John left them to go back to Jerusalem. ¹⁴The others carried on from Perga till they

ACTS 13:15

reached Antioch in Pisidia. Here they went to synagogue on the sabbath and took their seats. [15]After the lessons from the Law and the Prophets had been read, the presidents of the synagogue sent them a message: 'Brothers, if you would like to address some words of encouragement to the congregation, please do so'. [16]Paul stood up, held up a hand for silence and began to speak:

Paul's preaching before the Jews

'Men of Israel, and fearers of God, listen! [17]The God of our nation Israel chose our ancestors, and made our people great when they were living as foreigners in Egypt; then by divine power he led them out, [18]and for about forty years took care of them in the wilderness. [19]When he had destroyed seven nations in Canaan, he put them in possession[a] of their land [20]for about four hundred and fifty years. After this he gave them judges, down to the prophet Samuel. [21]Then they demanded a king, and God gave them Saul son of Kish, a man of the tribe of [22]Benjamin. After forty years, he deposed him and made David their king, of whom he approved in these words, "I have selected David son of Jesse, a man after my own heart, who will carry out my whole purpose".[b] [23]To keep his promise, God has raised up for Israel one of David's descendants, Jesus, as Saviour, [24]whose coming was heralded by John when he

---

[13a.] Dt 1:31; 7:1
[13b.] 1 S 13:14

proclaimed a baptism of repentance for the whole people of Israel. [25]Before John ended his career he said, "I am not the one you imagine me to be; that one is coming after me and I am not fit to undo his sandal". [26]My brothers, sons of Abraham's race, and all you who fear God, this message of salvation is meant for you. [27]What the people of Jerusalem and their rulers did, though they did not realise it, was in fact to fulfil the prophecies read on every sabbath. [28]Though they found nothing to justify his death, they condemned him and asked Pilate to have him executed. [29]When they had carried out everything that scripture foretells about him they took him down from the tree and buried him in a tomb. [30]But God raised him from the dead, [31]and for many days he appeared to those who had accompanied him from Galilee to Jerusalem: and it is these same companions of his who are now his witnesses before our people. [32]We have come here to tell you the Good News. It was to our ancestors that God made the promise but [33]it is to us, their children, that he has fulfilled it, by raising Jesus from the dead. As scripture says in the first psalm: "You are my son: today I have become your father." [34]The fact that God raised him from the dead, never to return to corruption, is no more than what he had declared: "To you I shall give the sure and holy things promised to David."[c] [35]This is explained by

---

[13c] Is 55:3

another text: "You will not allow your holy one to experience corruption."[d] 36Now when David in his own time had served God's purposes he died; he was buried with his ancestors and has certainly experienced corruption. 37The one whom God has raised up, however, has not experienced corruption. 38My brothers, I want you to realise that it is through him that forgiveness of your sins is proclaimed. Through him justification from all sins which the Law of Moses was unable to justify 39is offered to every believer. 40So be careful - or what the prophets say will happen to you. 41"Cast your eyes around you, mockers; be amazed, and perish! For I am doing something in your own days that you would not believe if you were to be told of it."[e] 42As they left they were asked to preach on the same theme the following sabbath. 43When the meeting broke up many Jews and devout converts joined Paul and Barnabas and in their talks with them Paul and Barnabas urged them to remain faithful to the grace God had given them.

Paul and Barnabas preach to the pagans

44The next sabbath almost the whole town assembled to hear the word of God. 45When they saw the crowds, the Jews, prompted by jealousy, used blasphemies and contradicted everything Paul said. 46Then Paul and Barnabas spoke out boldly. 'We had to proclaim the word

---

13 d. Ps 16:9
13 e. Hab 1:5

of God to you first, but since you have rejected it, since you do not think yourselves worthy of eternal life, we must turn to the pagans. [47]For this is what the Lord commanded us to do when he said: "I have made you a light for the nations, so that my salvation may reach the ends of the earth."[f] [48]It made the pagans very happy to hear this and they thanked the Lord for his message; all who were destined for eternal life became believers. [49]Thus the word of the Lord spread through the whole countryside. [50]But the Jews worked upon some of the devout women of the upper classes and the leading men of the city and persuaded them to turn against Paul and Barnabas and expel them from their territory. [51]So they shook the dust from their feet in defiance and went off to Iconium; [52]but the disciples were filled with joy and the Holy Spirit.

Iconium evangelised

14 [1]At Iconium they went to the Jewish synagogue, as they had at Antioch, and they spoke so effectively that a great many Jews and Greeks became believers. [2]Some of the Jews, however, refused to believe, and they poisoned the minds of the pagans against the brothers.[a] [3]Accordingly Paul and Barnabas stayed on for some time, preaching fearlessly for the Lord; and the Lord supported all they said about his gift of grace, allowing signs and

---

[13f.] Is 49:6, quoted freely from the LXX.
[14a.] This sentence is a parenthesis. v.3 continues from v.1.

wonders to be performed by them. [4]The people in the city were divided, some supported the Jews, others the apostles, [5]but eventually with the connivance of the authorities a move was made by pagans as well as Jews to make attacks on them and to stone them. [6]When the apostles came to hear of this, they went off for safety to Lycaonia where, in the towns of Lystra and Derbe and in the surrounding country, [7]they preached the Good News.

Healing of a cripple

[8]A man sat there[b] who had never walked in his life, because his feet were crippled from birth; [9]and as he listened to Paul preaching, he managed to catch his eye. Seeing that the man had the faith to be cured, [10]Paul said in a loud voice, 'Get to your feet - stand up', and the cripple jumped up and began to walk. [11]When the crowd saw what Paul had done they shouted in the language of Lycaonia, 'These people are gods who have come down to us disguised as men'. [12]They addressed Barnabas as Zeus, and since Paul was the principal speaker they called him Hermes.[c] [13]The priests of Zeus-outside-the-Gate, proposing that all the people should offer sacrifice with them, brought garlanded oxen to the gates. [14]When the apostles Barnabas and Paul heard what was happening they tore their clothes,[d] and rushed into the

---

14 b. In Lystra.

14 c. Mercury, the messenger or herald of the gods.

14 d. Conventional sign of despair.

crowd, shouting, [15]'Friends, what do you think you are doing? We are only human beings like you. We have come with good news to make you turn from these empty idols to the living God who made heaven and earth and the sea and all that these hold. [16]In the past he allowed each nation to go its own way; [17]but even then he did not leave you without evidence of himself in the good things he does for you: he sends you rain from heaven, he makes your crops grow when they should, he gives you food and makes you happy.' [18]Even this speech, however, was scarcely enough to stop the crowd offering them sacrifice.

The mission is disrupted

[19]Then some Jews arrived from Antioch and Iconium, and turned the people against the apostles. They stoned Paul and dragged him outside the town, thinking he was dead. [20]The disciples came crowding round him but, as they did so, he stood up and went back to the town. The next day he and Barnabas went off to Derbe. [21]Having preached the Good News in that town and made a considerable number of disciples, they went back through Lystra and Iconium to Antioch. [22]They put fresh heart into the disciples, encouraging them to persevere in the faith. 'We all have to experience many hardships' they said 'before we enter the kingdom of God.' [23]In each of these churches they appointed elders, and with prayer and fasting they commended them to the Lord in whom they had come to

believe. [24]They passed through Pisidia and reached Pamphylia. [25]Then after proclaiming the word at Perga they went down to Attalia [26]and from there sailed for Antioch, where they had originally been commended to the grace of God for the work they had now completed. [27]On their arrival they assembled the church and gave an account of all that God had done with them, and how he had opened the door of faith to the pagans. [28]They stayed there with the disciples for some time.

Controversy at Antioch

15 [1]Then some men came down from Judaea[a] and taught the brothers, 'Unless you have yourselves circumcised in the tradition of Moses you cannot be saved'. [2]This led to disagreement, and after Paul and Barnabas had had a long argument with these men it was arranged that Paul and Barnabas and others of the church should go up to Jerusalem and discuss the problem with the apostles and elders. [3]All the members of the church saw them off, and as they passed through Phoenicia and Samaria they told how the pagans had been converted, and this news was received with the greatest satisfaction by the brothers. [4]When they arrived in Jerusalem they were welcomed by the church and by the apostles and elders, and gave an account of all that God had done with them.

[15a]. In the allusion to this incident in Ga, they are said to have come 'from James', Ga 2:12.

Controversy at Jerusalem

⁵But certain members of the Pharisees' party who had become believers objected, insisting that the pagans should be circumcised and instructed to keep the Law of Moses. ⁶The apostles and elders met to look into the matter, ⁷and after the discussion had gone on a long time, Peter stood up and addressed them.

Peter's speech

'My brothers,' he said 'you know perfectly well that in the early days God made his choice among you: the pagans were to learn the Good News from me and so become believers. ⁸In fact God, who can read everyone's heart, showed his approval of them by giving the Holy Spirit to them just as he had to us. ⁹God made no distinction between them and us, since he purified their hearts by faith. ¹⁰It would only provoke God's anger now, surely, if you imposed on the disciples the very burden that neither we nor our ancestors were strong enough to support? ¹¹Remember, we believe that we are saved in the same way as they are: through the grace of the Lord Jesus.' ¹²This silenced the entire assembly, and they listened to Barnabas and Paul describing the signs and wonders God had worked through them among the pagans.

James' speech

¹³When they had finished it was James who spoke. 'My brothers,' he said 'listen to me. ¹⁴Simeonᵇ has described how God first arranged to enlist a people for his name out of the pagans. ¹⁵This is entirely in harmony with the words of the prophets, since the scriptures say: ¹⁶"After that I shall return and rebuild the fallen House of David; I shall rebuild it from its ruins and restore it. ¹⁷Then the rest of mankind, all the pagans who are consecrated to my name, will look for the Lord, says the Lord who made this ¹⁸known so long ago."ᶜ ¹⁹'I rule, then, that instead of making things more difficult for pagans who turn to God, ²⁰we send them a letter telling them merely to abstain from anything polluted by idols,ᵈ from fornication,ᵉ from the meat of strangled animals and from blood. ²¹For Moses has always had his preachers in every town, and is read aloud in the synagogues every sabbath.'

The apostolic letter

²²Then the apostles and elders decided to choose delegates to send to Antioch with Paul and Barnabas; the whole church concurred with this. They chose Judas known as Barsabbas and Silas,ᶠ both leading men in the brotherhood, ²³and gave

---

¹⁵ᵇ Semitic form of Simon Peter's name.
¹⁵ᶜ Am 9:11, 12, quoted according to the LXX.
¹⁵ᵈ I.e. which has been offered in sacrifice to false gods.
¹⁵ᵉ Perhaps all the irregular marriages listed in Lv 18.
¹⁵ᶠ Silas, also mentioned in Ac 18; 1 Th, 2 Th, 2 Co, 1 P.

them this letter to take with them: 'The apostles and elders, your brothers, send greetings to the brothers of pagan birth in Antioch, Syria and Cilicia. [24]We hear that some of our members have disturbed you with their demands and have unsettled your minds. They acted without any authority from us; [25]and so we have decided unanimously to elect delegates and to send them to you with Barnabas and Paul, men we highly respect [26]who have dedicated their lives to the name of our Lord Jesus Christ. [27]Accordingly we are sending you Judas and Silas, who will confirm by word of mouth what we have written in this letter. [28]It has been decided by the Holy Spirit and by ourselves not to saddle you with any burden beyond these essentials: [29]you are to abstain from food sacrificed to idols; from blood, from the meat of strangled animals and from fornication. Avoid these, and you will do what is right. Farewell.'

The delegates at Antioch

[30]The party left and went down to Antioch, where they summoned the whole community and delivered the letter. [31]The community read it and were delighted with the encouragement it gave them. [32]Judas and Silas, being themselves prophets, spoke for a long time, encouraging and strengthening the brothers. [33]These two spent some time there, and then the brothers wished them peace and they went back to those who had sent them. [35]Paul and Barnabas, however, stayed on

in Antioch, and there with many others they taught and proclaimed the Good News, the word of the Lord.

IV. PAUL'S MISSIONS

Paul separates from Barnabas and recruits Silas

³⁶On a later occasion Paul said to Barnabas, 'Let us go back and visit all the towns where we preached the word of the Lord, so that we can see how the brothers are doing'. ³⁷Barnabas suggested taking John Mark, ³⁸but Paul was not in favour of taking along the very man who had deserted them in Pamphylia and had refused to share in their work. ³⁹After a violent quarrel they parted company, and Barnabas sailed off with Mark to Cyprus. ⁴⁰Before Paul left, he chose Silas to accompany him and was commended by the brothers to the grace of God.

Lycaonia: Paul recruits Timothy

⁴¹He travelled through Syria and Cilicia, consolidating the churches.

16 ¹From there he went to Derbe, and then on to Lystra. Here there was a disciple called Timothy, whose mother was a Jewess who had become a believer; but his father was a Greek. ²The brothers at Lystra and Iconium spoke well of Timothy, ³and Paul, who wanted to have him as a travelling companion, had him circumcised. This was on account of the Jews in the locality where everyone knew his father was a Greek. ⁴As they visited one town after another, they passed on the decisions reached by the apostles and elders in Jerusalem, with instructions to respect them. ⁵So the churches grew strong in the faith, as well as growing daily in numbers.

The crossing into Asia Minor

⁶They travelled through Phrygia and the Galatian country, having been told by the Holy Spirit not to preach the word in Asia. ⁷When they reached the frontier of Mysia they thought to cross it into Bithynia, but as the Spirit of Jesus would not allow them, ⁸they went through Mysia and came down to Troas. ⁹One night Paul had a vision: a Macedonian appeared and appealed to him in these words, 'Come across to Macedonia and help us'. ¹⁰Once he had seen this vision we lost no time in arranging a passage to Macedonia, convinced that God had called us to bring them the Good News.

Arrival at Philippi

¹¹Sailing from Troas we made a straight run for Samothrace; the next day for Neapolis, ¹²and from there for Philippi, a Roman colony and the principal city of that particular district of Macedonia. After a few days in this city ¹³we went along the river outside the gates as it was the sabbath and this was a customary place for prayer.ª We sat down and preached to the women who had come to the meeting. ¹⁴One of these women was called Lydia, a devout

¹⁶ª There was no synagogue in this Latin city; the Jews met by the river for ritual ablutions.

woman from the town of Thyatira who was in the purple-dye trade. She listened to us, and the Lord opened her heart to accept what Paul was saying. [15]After she and her household had been baptised she sent us an invitation: 'If you really think me a true believer in the Lord,' she said 'come and stay with us'; and she would take no refusal.

Imprisonment of Paul and Silas

[16]One day as we were going to prayer, we met a slave-girl who was a soothsayer and made a lot of money for her masters by telling fortunes. [17]This girl started following Paul and the rest of us and shouting, 'Here are the servants of the Most High God; they have come to tell you how to be saved!' [18]She did this every day afterwards until Paul lost his temper one day and turned round and said to the spirit, 'I order you in the name of Jesus Christ to leave that woman'. The spirit went out of her then and there. [19]When her masters saw that there was no hope of making any more money out of her, they seized Paul and Silas and dragged them to the law courts in the market place [20]where they charged them before the magistrates and said, 'These people are causing a disturbance in our city. They are Jews [21]and are advocating practices which it is unlawful for us as Romans to accept or follow.'[b] [22]The crowd joined in and showed their hostility to them, so the magistrates had them stripped and ordered them to be flogged. [23]They

---

[16 b.] The Jews had no right to proselytise Romans.

were given many lashes and then thrown into prison, and the gaoler was told to keep a close watch on them. ²⁴So, following his instructions, he threw them into the inner prison and fastened their feet in the stocks.

The miraculous deliverance of Paul and Silas

²⁵Late that night Paul and Silas were praying and singing God's praises, while the other prisoners listened. ²⁶Suddenly there was an earthquake that shook the prison to its foundations. All the doors flew open and the chains fell from all the prisoners. ²⁷When the gaoler woke and saw the doors wide open he drew his sword and was about to commit suicide, presuming that the prisoners had escaped. ²⁸But Paul shouted at the top of his voice, 'Don't do yourself any harm; we are all here'. ²⁹The gaoler called for lights, then rushed in, threw himself trembling at the feet of Paul and Silas, ³⁰and escorted them out, saying, 'Sirs, what must I do to be saved?' ³¹They told him, 'Become a believer in the Lord Jesus, and you will be saved, and your household too'. ³²Then they preached the word of the Lord to him and to all his family. ³³Late as it was, he took them to wash their wounds, and was baptised then and there with all his household. ³⁴Afterwards he took them home and gave them a meal, and the whole family celebrated their conversion to belief in God. ³⁵When it was daylight the magistrates sent the officers with the order: 'Release those men'. ³⁶The gaoler

reported the message to Paul, 'The magistrates have sent an order for your release; you can go now and be on your way'. [37]'What!' Paul replied 'They flog Roman citizens in public and without trial and throw us into prison, and then think they can push us out on the quiet! Oh no! They must come and escort us out themselves.' [38]The officers reported this to the magistrates, who were horrified to hear the men were Roman citizens. [39]They came and begged them to leave the town. From the prison they went to Lydia's house where they saw all the brothers and gave them some encouragement; then they left.

Thessalonika: difficulties with the Jews

17 [1]Passing through Amphipolis and Apollonia, they eventually reached Thessalonika, where there was a Jewish synagogue. [2]Paul as usual introduced himself and for three consecutive sabbaths developed the arguments from scripture for them, [3]explaining and proving how it was ordained that the Christ should suffer and rise from the dead. 'And the Christ' he said 'is this Jesus whom I am proclaiming to you.' [4]Some of them were convinced and joined Paul and Silas, and so did a great many God-fearing people and Greeks, as well as a number of rich women. [5]The Jews, full of resentment, enlisted the help of a gang from the market place, stirred up a crowd, and soon had the whole city in an uproar. They made for Jason's house, hoping to find them there and drag them off to the

68

People's Assembly; [6]however, they only found Jason and some of the brothers, and these they dragged before the city council, shouting, 'The people who have been turning the whole world upside down have come here now; [7]they have been staying at Jason's. They have broken every one of Caesar's edicts by claiming that there is another emperor, Jesus.' [8]This accusation alarmed the citizens and the city councillors [9]and they made Jason and the rest give security before setting them free.

Fresh difficulties at Beroea

[10]When it was dark the brothers immediately sent Paul and Silas away to Beroea, where they visited the Jewish synagogue as soon as they arrived. [11]Here the Jews were more open-minded than those in Thessalonika, and they welcomed the word very readily; every day they studied the scriptures to check whether it was true. [12]Many Jews became believers, and so did many Greek women from the upper classes and a number of the men. [13]When the Jews of Thessalonika heard that the word of God was being preached by Paul in Beroea as well, they went there to make trouble and stir up the people. [14]So the brothers arranged for Paul to go immediately as far as the coast, leaving Silas and Timothy behind. [15]Paul's escort took him as far as Athens, and went back with instructions for Silas and Timothy to rejoin Paul as soon as they could.

Paul in Athens

[16]Paul waited for them in Athens and there his whole soul was revolted at the sight of a city given over to idolatry. [17]In the synagogue he held debates with the Jews and the God-fearing, but in the market place he had debates every day with anyone who would face him. [18]Even a few Epicurean and Stoic philosophers argued with him. Some said, 'Does this parrot know what he's talking about?' And, because he was preaching about Jesus and the resurrection, others said, 'He sounds like a propagandist for some outlandish gods'.[a] [19]They invited him to accompany them to the Council of the Areopagus, where they said to him, 'How much of this new teaching you were speaking about are we allowed to know? [20]Some of the things you said seemed startling to us and we would like to find out what they mean.' [21]The one amusement the Athenians and the foreigners living there seem to have, apart from discussing the latest ideas, is listening to lectures about them. [22]So Paul stood before the whole Council of the Areopagus and made this speech:

Paul's speech before the Council of the Areopagus

'Men of Athens, I have seen for myself how extremely scrupulous you are in all religious matters, [23]because I noticed, as I strolled round admiring your sacred

---

[17 a.] They assumed that *Anastasis* ('Resurrection') was the name of a goddess.

monuments, that you had an altar inscribed: To An Unknown God. Well, the God whom I proclaim is in fact the one whom you already worship without knowing it. [24]Since the God who made the world and everything in it is himself Lord of heaven and earth, he does not make his home in shrines made by human hands. [25]Nor is he dependent on anything that human hands can do for him, since he can never be in need of anything; on the contrary, it is he who gives everything - including life and breath - to everyone. [26]From one single stock he not only created the whole human race so that they could occupy the entire earth, but he decreed how long each nation should flourish and what the boundaries of its territory should be. [27]And he did this so that all nations might seek the deity and, by feeling their way towards him, succeed in finding him. Yet in fact he is not far from any of us, [28]since it is in him that we live, and move, and exist,[b] as indeed some of your own writers have said: "We are all his children".[c] [29]Since we are the children of God, we have no excuse for thinking that the deity looks like anything in gold, silver or stone that has been carved and designed by a man. [30]God overlooked that sort of thing when men were ignorant, but now he is telling everyone everywhere that they must repent, [31]because he has fixed a day when the whole world will be judged, and judged in righteousness, and he has

---

17[b]. Expression suggested by the poet Epimenides.

17[c]. From the *Phainomena* of Aratus.

appointed a man to be the judge. And God has publicly proved this by raising this man from the dead.' ³²At this mention of rising from the dead, some of them burst out laughing; others said, 'We would like to hear you talk about this again'. ³³After that Paul left them, ³⁴but there were some who attached themselves to him and became believers, among them Dionysius the Areopagite and a woman called Damaris, and others besides.

Foundation of the church of Corinth

18 ¹After this Paul left Athens and went to Corinth, ²where he met a Jew called Aquila whose family came from Pontus. He and his wife Priscilla[a] had recently left Italy because an edict of Claudius had expelled all the Jews from Rome.[b] Paul went to visit them, ³and when he found they were tentmakers, of the same trade as himself, he lodged with them, and they worked together. ⁴Every sabbath he used to hold debates in the synagogues, trying to convert Jews as well as Greeks. ⁵After Silas and Timothy had arrived from Macedonia, Paul devoted all his time to preaching, declaring to the Jews that Jesus was the Christ. ⁶When they turned against him and started to insult him, he took his cloak and shook it out in front of them, saying, 'Your blood be on your own heads; from now on I can go to the pagans with a clear conscience'. ⁷Then he left the synagogue and

---

18 a. Also called Prisca, Rm 16:3; 1 Co 16:19; 2 Tm 4:19.
18 b. This edict was issued in 49 or 50.

moved to the house next door that belonged to a worshipper of God called Justus. [8]Crispus, president of the synagogue, and his whole household, all became believers in the Lord. A great many Corinthians who had heard him became believers and were baptised. [9]One night the Lord spoke to Paul in a vision, 'Do not be afraid to speak out, nor allow yourself to be silenced: [10]I am with you. I have so many people on my side in this city that no one will even attempt to hurt you.' [11]So Paul stayed there preaching the word of God among them for eighteen months.

The Jews take Paul to court

[12]But while Gallio was proconsul of Achaia,[c] the Jews made a concerted attack on Paul and brought him before the tribunal. [13]'We accuse this man' they said 'of persuading people to worship God in a way that breaks the Law.' [14]Before Paul could open his mouth, Gallio said to the Jews, 'Listen, you Jews. If this were a misdemeanour or a crime, I would not hesitate to attend to you; [15]but if it is only quibbles about words and names, and about your own Law, then you must deal with it yourselves - I have no intention of making legal decisions about things like that.' [16]Then he sent them out of the court, [17]and at once they all turned on Sosthenes, the synagogue president, and beat him in front of the court house. Gallio refused to take any notice at all.

[18 c.] In 52, according to an inscription from Delphi.

Return to Antioch and departure for the third journey

[18]After staying on for some time, Paul took leave of the brothers and sailed for Syria,[d] accompanied by Priscilla and Aquila. At Cenchreae he had his hair cut off, because of a vow he had made. [19]When they reached Ephesus, he left them, but first he went alone to the synagogue to debate with the Jews. [20]They asked him to stay longer but he declined, though when he left he said, 'I will come back another time, God willing'. Then he sailed from Ephesus. [22]He landed at Caesarea, and went up to greet the church. Then he came down to Antioch [23]where he spent a short time before continuing his journey through the Galatian country and then through Phrygia, encouraging all the followers.

Apollos

[24]An Alexandrian Jew named Apollos now arrived in Ephesus. He was an eloquent man, with a sound knowledge of the scriptures, and yet, [25]though he had been given instruction in the Way of the Lord and preached with great spiritual earnestness and was accurate in all the details he taught about Jesus, he had only experienced the baptism of John. [26]When Priscilla and Aquila heard him speak boldly in the synagogue, they took an interest in him and gave him further instruction about the Way. [27]When Apollos thought of

---

[18] d. To Antioch.

crossing over to Achaia, the brothers encouraged him and wrote asking the disciples to welcome him. When he arrived there he was able by God's grace to help the believers considerably ²⁸by the energetic way he refuted the Jews in public and demonstrated from the scriptures that Jesus was the Christ.

The disciples of John at Ephesus

19 ¹While Apollos was in Corinth, Paul made his way overland as far as Ephesus, where he found a number of disciples. ²When he asked, 'Did you receive the Holy Spirit when you became believers?' they answered, 'No, we were never even told there was such a thing as a Holy Spirit'. ³'Then how were you baptised?' he asked. 'With John's baptism' they replied. ⁴'John's baptism' said Paul 'was a baptism of repentance; but he insisted that the people should believe in the one who was to come after him - in other words Jesus.' ⁵When they heard this, they were baptised in the name of the Lord Jesus, ⁶and the moment Paul had laid hands on them the Holy Spirit came down on them, and they began to speak with tongues and to prophesy. ⁷There were about twelve of these men.

Foundation of the church of Ephesus

⁸He began by going to the synagogue, where he spoke out boldly and argued persuasively about the kingdom of God. He did this for three months, ⁹till the attitude of some of the congregation hardened into unbelief. As soon as they began

attacking the Way in front of the others, he broke with them and took his disciples apart to hold daily discussions in the lecture room of Tyrannus. [10]This went on for two years, with the result that people from all over Asia,[a] both Jews and Greeks, were able to hear the word of the Lord.

The Jewish exorcists

[11]So remarkable were the miracles worked by God at Paul's hands [12]that handkerchiefs or aprons which had touched him were taken to the sick, and they were cured of their illnesses, and the evil spirits came out of them. [13]But some itinerant Jewish exorcists tried pronouncing the name of the Lord Jesus over people who were possessed by evil spirits; they used to say, 'I command you by the Jesus whose spokesman is Paul'. [14]Among those who did this were seven sons of Sceva, a Jewish chief priest. [15]The evil spirit replied, 'Jesus I recognise, and I know who Paul is, but who are you?' [16]and the man with the evil spirit hurled himself at them and overpowered first one and then another, and handled them so violently that they fled from that house naked and badly mauled. [17]Everybody in Ephesus, both Jews and Greeks, heard about this episode; they were all greatly impressed, and the name of the Lord Jesus came to be held in great honour. [18]Some believers, too, came forward to admit in detail how they had used spells [19]and a number

---

[19a]. I.e. the region round Ephesus, including the seven towns of Rv 1:11

of them who had practised magic collected their books and made a bonfire of them in public. The value of these was calculated to be fifty thousand silver pieces. [20]In this impressive way the word of the Lord spread more and more widely and successfully.

V. A PRISONER FOR CHRIST

Paul's plans

[21]When all this was over Paul made up his mind to go back to Jerusalem through Macedonia and Achaia. 'After I have been there' he said 'I must go on to see Rome as well.' [22]So he sent two of his helpers, Timothy and Erastus, ahead of him to Macedonia, while he remained for a time in Asia.

Ephesus: the silversmiths' riot

[23]It was during this time that a rather serious disturbance broke out in connection with the Way. [24]A silversmith called Demetrius, who employed a large number of craftsmen making silver shrines of Diana, [25]called a general meeting of his own men with others in the same trade. 'As you men know,' he said 'it is on this industry that we depend for our prosperity. [26]Now you must have seen and heard how, not just in Ephesus but nearly everywhere in Asia, this man Paul has persuaded and converted a great number of people with his argument that gods made by hand are not gods at all. [27]This threatens not only to discredit our trade, but also to reduce the sanctuary

of the great goddess Diana to unimportance. It could end up by taking away all the prestige of a goddess venerated all over Asia, yes, and everywhere in the civilised world.' [28]This speech roused them to fury, and they started to shout, 'Great is Diana of the Ephesians!' [29]The whole town was in an uproar and the mob rushed to the theatre dragging along two of Paul's Macedonian travelling companions, Gaius and Aristarchus. [30]Paul wanted to make an appeal to the people, but the disciples refused to let him; [31]in fact, some of the Asiarchs,[b] who were friends of his, sent messages imploring him not to take the risk of going into the theatre. [32]By now everybody was shouting different things till the assembly itself had no idea what was going on; most of them did not even know why they had been summoned. [33]The Jews pushed Alexander to the front, and when some of the crowd shouted encouragement he raised his hand for silence in the hope of being able to explain things to the people. [34]When they realised he was a Jew, they all started shouting in unison, 'Great is Diana of the Ephesians!' and they kept this up for two hours. [35]When the town clerk eventually succeeded in calming the crowd, he said, 'Citizens of Ephesus! Is there anybody alive who does not know that the city of the Ephesians is the guardian of the temple of great Diana and of her statue that fell from heaven? [36]Nobody can

---

[19 b.] Local leaders of the official state worship.

contradict this and there is no need for you to get excited or do anything rash. ³⁷These men you have brought here are not guilty of any sacrilege or blasphemy against our goddess. ³⁸If Demetrius and the craftsmen he has with him want to complain about anyone, there are the assizes and the proconsuls; let them take the case to court. ³⁹And if you want to ask any more questions you must raise them in the regular assembly. ⁴⁰We could easily be charged with rioting for today's happenings: there was no ground for it all, and we can give no reason for this gathering.' ⁴¹When he had finished this speech he dismissed the assembly.

Paul leaves Ephesus

20 ¹When the disturbance was over, Paul sent for the disciples and, after speaking words of encouragement to them, said good-bye and set out for Macedonia. ²On his way through those areas he said many words of encouragement to them and then made his way into Greece, ³where he spent three months. He was leaving by ship for Syria[a] when a plot organised against him by the Jews made him decide to go back by way of Macedonia. ⁴He was accompanied by Sopater, son of Pyrrhus, who came from Beroea; Aristarchus and Secundus who came from Thessalonika; Gaius from Doberus, and Timothy, as well as Tychicus and Trophimus who were from Asia. ⁵They all went on to Troas where they waited for us. ⁶We

---

20a. Taking to Jerusalem the proceeds of the collection, Rm 15:25.

ourselves left Philippi by ship after the days of Unleavened Bread and met them five days later at Troas, where we stopped for a week.

Troas: Paul raises a dead man to life

[7]On the first day of the week[b] we met to break bread. Paul was due to leave the next day, and he preached a sermon that went on till the middle of the night. [8]A number of lamps were lit in the upstairs room where we were assembled, [9]and as Paul went on and on, a young man called Eutychus who was sitting on the window-sill grew drowsy and was overcome by sleep and fell to the ground three floors below. He was picked up dead. [10]Paul went down and stooped to clasp the boy to him. 'There is no need to worry,' he said 'there is still life in him.' [11]Then he went back upstairs where he broke bread and ate and carried on talking till he left at daybreak. [12]They took the boy away alive, and were greatly encouraged.

From Troas to Miletus

[13]We were now to go on ahead by sea, so we set sail for Assos, where we were to take Paul on board; this was what he had arranged, for he wanted to go by road. [14]When he rejoined us at Assos we took him aboard and went on to Mitylene. [15]The next day we sailed from there and arrived opposite Chios. The second day we touched at

---

[20 b.] The day was reckoned in the Jewish fashion; the Lord's day began on the evening of Saturday and it was then that this meeting was held.

Samos and, after stopping at Trogyllium, made Miletus the next day. ¹⁶Paul had decided to pass wide of Ephesus so as to avoid spending time in Asia, since he was anxious to be in Jerusalem, if possible, for the day of Pentecost.

Farewell to the elders of Ephesus

¹⁷From Miletus he sent for the elders of the church of Ephesus. ¹⁸When they arrived he addressed these words to them: 'You know what my way of life has been ever since the first day I set foot among you in Asia, ¹⁹how I have served the Lord in all humility, with all the sorrows and trials that came to me through the plots of the Jews. ²⁰I have not hesitated to do anything that would be helpful to you; I have preached to you, and instructed you both in public and in your homes, ²¹urging both Jews and Greeks to turn to God and to believe in our Lord Jesus. ²²And now you see me a prisoner already in spirit; I am on my way to Jerusalem, but have no idea what will happen to me there, ²³except that the Holy Spirit, in town after town, has made it clear enough that imprisonment and persecution await me. ²⁴But life to me is not a thing to waste words on, provided that when I finish my race I have carried out the mission the Lord Jesus gave me - and that was to bear witness to the Good News of God's grace. ²⁵I now feel sure that none of you among whom I have gone about proclaiming the kingdom will ever see my face again. ²⁶And so here and now I swear that my

conscience is clear as far as all of you are concerned, [27]for I have without faltering put before you the whole of God's purpose. [28]Be on your guard for yourselves and for all the flock of which the Holy Spirit has made you the overseers, to feed the Church of God which he bought with his own blood. [29]I know quite well that when I have gone fierce wolves will invade you and will have no mercy on the flock. [30]Even from your own ranks there will be men coming forward with a travesty of the truth on their lips to induce the disciples to follow them. [31]So be on your guard, remembering how night and day for three years I never failed to keep you right, shedding tears over each one of you. [32]And now I commend you to God, and to the word of his grace that has power to build you up and to give you your inheritance among all the sanctified. [33]I have never asked anyone for money or clothes; [34]you know for yourselves that the work I did earned enough to meet my needs and those of my companions. [35]I did this to show you that this is how we must exert ourselves to support the weak, remembering the words of the Lord Jesus, who himself said, "There is more happiness in giving than in receiving".' [36]When he had finished speaking he knelt down with them all and prayed. [37]By now they were all in tears; they put their arms round Paul's neck and kissed him; [38]what saddened them most was his saying they would never see his face again. Then they escorted him to the ship.

The Journey to Jerusalem

21 ¹When we had at last torn ourselves away from them and put to sea, we set a straight course and arrived at Cos; the next day we reached Rhodes, and from there went on to Patara. ²Here we found a ship bound for Phoenicia, so we went on board and sailed in her. ³After sighting Cyprus and leaving it to port, we sailed to Syria and put in at Tyre, since the ship was to unload her cargo there. ⁴We sought out the disciples and stayed there a week. Speaking in the Spirit, they kept telling Paul not to go on to Jerusalem, ⁵but when our time was up we set off. Together with the women and children they all escorted us on our way till we were out of the town. When we reached the beach, we knelt down and prayed; ⁶then, after saying good-bye to each other, we went aboard and they returned home. ⁷The end of our voyage from Tyre came when we landed at Ptolemais, where we greeted the brothers and stayed one day with them. ⁸The next day we left and came to Caesarea. Here we called on Philip the evangelist, one of the Seven, and stayed with him. ⁹He had four virgin daughters who were prophets. ¹⁰When we had been there several days a prophet called Agabus arrived from Judaea ¹¹to see us. He took Paul's girdle, and tied up his own feet and hands, and said, 'This is what the Holy Spirit says, "The man this girdle belongs to will be bound like this by the Jews in Jerusalem, and handed over to the pagans"'. ¹²When we heard this, we and everybody there implored

Paul not to go on to Jerusalem. [13]To this he replied, 'What are you trying to do - weaken my resolution by your tears? For my part, I am ready not only to be tied up but even to die in Jerusalem for the name of the Lord Jesus.' [14]And so, as he would not be persuaded, we gave up the attempt, saying, 'The Lord's will be done'.

Paul's arrival in Jerusalem

[15]After this we packed and went on up to Jerusalem. [16]Some of the disciples from Caesarea accompanied us and took us to the house of a Cypriot with whom we were to lodge; he was called Mnason and had been one of the earliest disciples. [17]On our arrival in Jerusalem the brothers gave us a very warm welcome. [18]The next day Paul went with us to visit James, and all the elders were present. [19]After greeting them he gave a detailed account of all that God had done among the pagans through his ministry. [20]They gave glory to God when they heard this. 'But you see, brother,' they said 'how thousands of Jews have now become believers, all of them staunch upholders of the Law, and [21]they have heard that you instruct all Jews living among the pagans to break away from Moses, authorising them not to circumcise their children or to follow the customary practices. [22]What is to be done? Inevitably there will be a meeting of the whole body, since they are bound to hear that you have come. [23]So do as we suggest. We have four men here who are

under a vow; [24]take these men along and be purified with them and pay all the expenses connected with the shaving of their heads.[a] This will let everyone know there is no truth in the reports they have heard about you and that you still regularly observe the Law. [25]The pagans who have become believers, as we wrote when we told them our decisions, must abstain from things sacrificed to idols, from blood, from the meat of strangled animals and from fornication.' [26]So the next day Paul took the men along and was purified with them and he visited the Temple to give notice of the time when the period of purification would be over and the offering would have to be presented on behalf of each of them.

Paul's arrest

[27]The seven days were nearly over when some Jews from Asia caught sight of him in the Temple and stirred up the crowd and seized him, [28]shouting, 'Men of Israel, help! This is the man who preaches to everyone everywhere against our people, against the Law and against this place. Now he has profaned this Holy Place by bringing Greeks into the Temple.' [29]They had, in fact, previously seen Trophimus the Ephesian in the city with him, and thought that Paul had brought him into the Temple. [30]This roused

---

[21]a. For the duration of a nazirite vow, the hair was not to be cut. Discharge from the vow, on fulfilment, had to be celebrated with expensive sacrifices.

the whole city; people came running from all sides; they seized Paul and dragged him out of the Temple, and the gates were closed behind them. [31]They would have killed him if a report had not reached the tribune of the cohort[b] that there was rioting all over Jerusalem. [32]He immediately called out soldiers and centurions, and charged down on the crowd, who stopped beating Paul when they saw the tribune and the soldiers. [33]When the tribune came up he arrested Paul, had him bound with two chains and enquired who he was and what he had done. [34]People in the crowd called out different things, and since the noise made it impossible for him to get any positive information, the tribune ordered Paul to be taken into the fortress. [35]When Paul reached the steps, the crowd became so violent that he had to be carried by the soldiers; [36]and indeed the whole mob was after them, shouting, 'Kill him!' [37]Just as Paul was being taken into the fortress, he asked the tribune if he could have a word with him. The tribune said, 'You speak Greek, then? [38]So you are not the Egyptian who started the recent revolt and led those four thousand cut-throats[c] out into the desert?' [39]'I?' said Paul 'I am a Jew and a citizen of the well-known city of Tarsus in Cilicia. Please give me permission to speak to the people.' [40]The man gave his consent and Paul, standing at the top of the steps,

---

[21 b.] Commanding officer of the Roman garrison.
[21 c.] Nationalist extremists.

gestured to the people with his hand. When all was quiet again he spoke to them in Hebrew. [d]

Paul's address to the Jews of Jerusalem

22 '"My brothers, my fathers, listen to what I have to say to you in my defence.' [2]When they realised he was speaking in Hebrew, the silence was even greater than before. [3]'I am a Jew,' Paul said 'and was born at Tarsus in Cilicia. I was brought up here in this city. I studied under Gamaliel and was taught the exact observance of the Law of our ancestors. In fact, I was as full of duty towards God as you are today. [4]I even persecuted this Way to the death, and sent women as well as men to prison in chains [5]as the high priest and the whole council of elders can testify, since they even sent me with letters to their brothers in Damascus. When I set off it was with the intention of bringing prisoners back from there to Jerusalem for punishment. [6]I was on that journey and nearly at Damascus when about midday a bright light from heaven suddenly shone round me. [7]I fell to the ground and heard a voice saying, "Saul, Saul, why are you persecuting me?" [8]I answered: Who are you, Lord? and he said to me, "I am Jesus the Nazarene, and you are persecuting me". [9]The people with me saw the light but did not hear his voice as he spoke to me. [10]I said: What am I to do, Lord? The Lord answered, "Stand up

---

[21 d.] I.e. Aramaic.

and go into Damascus, and there you will be told what you have been appointed to do". [11]The light had been so dazzling that I was blind and my companions had to take me by the hand; and so I came to Damascus. [12]Someone called Ananias, a devout follower of the Law and highly thought of by all the Jews living there, [13]came to see me; he stood beside me and said, "Brother Saul, receive your sight". Instantly my sight came back and I was able to see him. [14]Then he said, "The God of our ancestors has chosen you to know his will, to see the Just One and hear his own voice speaking, [15]because you are to be his witness before all mankind, testifying to what you have seen and heard. [16]And now why delay? It is time you were baptised and had your sins washed away while invoking his name." [17]Once, after I had got back to Jerusalem, when I was praying in the Temple, I fell into a trance [18]and then I saw him. "Hurry," he said "leave Jerusalem at once; they will not accept the testimony you are giving about me" [19]Lord, I answered, it is because they know that I used to go from synagogue to synagogue, imprisoning and flogging those who believed in you; [20]and that when the blood of your witness[a] Stephen was being shed, I was standing by in full agreement with his murderers, and minding their clothes. [21]Then he said to me, "Go! I am sending you out to the pagans far away."'

[22a] *Martyr*: the word had not yet acquired its restricted meaning.

Paul the Roman citizen

[22]So far they had listened to him, but at these words they began to shout, 'Rid the earth of the man! He is not fit to live!' [23]They were yelling, waving their cloaks and throwing dust into the air, [24]and so the tribune had him brought into the fortress and ordered him to be examined under the lash, to find out the reason for the outcry against him. [25]But when they had strapped him down Paul said to the centurion on duty, 'Is it legal for you to flog a man who is a Roman citizen and has not been brought to trial?' [26]When he heard this the centurion went and told the tribune; 'Do you realise what you are doing?' he said 'This man is a Roman citizen'. [27]So the tribune came and asked him, 'Tell me, are you a Roman citizen?' 'I am' Paul said. [28]The tribune replied, 'It cost me a large sum to acquire this citizenship'. 'But I was born to it' said Paul. [29]Then those who were about to examine him hurriedly withdrew, and the tribune himself was alarmed when he realised that he had put a Roman citizen in chains.

His appearance before the Sanhedrin

[30]The next day, since he wanted to know what precise charge the Jews were bringing, he freed Paul and gave orders for a meeting of the chief priests and the entire Sanhedrin; then he brought Paul down and stood him in front of them.

23 [1]Paul looked steadily at the Sanhedrin and began to speak, 'My brothers, to this day I have conducted myself before God with a perfectly clear conscience'. [2]At this the high priest Ananias ordered his attendants to strike him on the mouth. [3]Then Paul said to him, 'God will surely strike you, you whitewashed wall! How can you sit there to judge me according to the Law, and then break the Law by ordering a man to strike me?' [4]The attendants said, 'It is God's high priest you are insulting!' [5]Paul answered, 'Brothers, I did not realise it was the high priest, for scripture says: "You must not curse a ruler of your people"'.[a] [6]Now Paul was well aware that one section was made up of Sadducees and the other of Pharisees, so he called out in the Sanhedrin, 'Brothers, I am a Pharisee and the son of Pharisees. It is for our hope in the resurrection of the dead that I am on trial.' [7]As soon as he said this a dispute broke out between the Pharisees and Sadducees, and the assembly was split between the two parties. [8]For the Sadducees say there is neither resurrection, nor angel, nor spirit, while the Pharisees accept all three. [9]The shouting grew louder, and some of the scribes from the Pharisees' party stood up and protested strongly, 'We find nothing wrong with this man. Suppose a spirit has spoken to him, or an angel?' [10]Feeling was running high, and the tribune, afraid that they would tear Paul to pieces, ordered his troops to go down and haul him out and bring him into the fortress.

[23 a.] Ex 22:27

¹¹Next night, the Lord appeared to him and said, 'Courage! You have borne witness for me in Jerusalem, now you must do the same in Rome.'

The conspiracy of the Jews against Paul

¹²When it was day, the Jews held a secret meeting at which they made a vow not to eat or drink until they had killed Paul. ¹³There were more than forty who took part in this conspiracy, ¹⁴and they went to the chief priests and elders, and told them, 'We have made a solemn vow to let nothing pass our lips until we have killed Paul. ¹⁵Now it is up to you and the Sanhedrin together to apply to the tribune to bring him down to you, as though you meant to examine his case more closely; we, on our side, are prepared to dispose of him before he reaches you.' ¹⁶But the son of Paul's sister heard of the ambush they were laying and made his way into the fortress and told Paul, ¹⁷who called one of the centurions and said, 'Take this young man to the tribune; he has something to tell him'. ¹⁸So the man took him to the tribune, and reported, 'The prisoner Paul summoned me and requested me to bring this young man to you; he has something to tell you'. ¹⁹Then the tribune took him by the hand and drew him aside and asked, 'What is it you have to tell me?' ²⁰He replied, 'The Jews have made a plan to ask you to take Paul down to the Sanhedrin tomorrow, as though they meant to inquire more closely into his case. ²¹Do not let

them persuade you. There are more than forty of them lying in wait for him, and they have vowed not to eat or drink until they have got rid of him. They are ready now and only waiting for your order to be given.' [22]The tribune let the young man go with this caution, 'Tell no one that you have given me this information'.

Paul transferred to Caesarea

[23]Then he summoned two of the centurions and said, 'Get two hundred soldiers ready to leave for Caesarea by the third hour of the night with seventy cavalry and two hundred auxiliaries; [24]provide horses for Paul, and deliver him unharmed to Felix the governor'.[b] [25]He also wrote a letter in these terms: [26]'Claudius Lysias to his Excellency the governor Felix, greetings. [27]This man had been seized by the Jews and would have been murdered by them but I came on the scene with my troops and got him away, having discovered that he was a Roman citizen. [28]Wanting to find out what charge they were making against him, I brought him before their Sanhedrin. [29]I found that the accusation concerned disputed points of their Law, but that there was no charge deserving death or imprisonment. [30]My information is that there is a conspiracy against the man, so I hasten to send him to you, and have notified his accusers that they must state their case against him in your presence.' [31]The soldiers carried out their orders; they took Paul and

---

[23 b.] Antoninus Felix, procurator of Judaea from 52 to 59-60.

escorted him by night to Antipatris. [32]Next day they left the mounted escort to go on with him and returned to the fortress. [33]On arriving at Caesarea the escort delivered the letter to the governor and handed Paul over to him. [34]The governor read the letter and asked him what province he came from. Learning that he was from Cilicia he said, [35]'I will hear your case as soon as your accusers are here too'. Then he ordered him to be held in Herod's praetorium.

The case before Felix

24 [1]Five days later the high priest Ananias came down with some of the elders and an advocate named Tertullus, and they laid information against Paul before the governor. [2]Paul was called, and Tertullus opened for the prosecution, 'Your Excellency, Felix, the unbroken peace we enjoy and the reforms this nation owes to your foresight [3]are matters we accept, always and everywhere, with all gratitude. [4]I do not want to take up too much of your time, but I beg you to give us a brief hearing. [5]The plain truth is that we find this man a perfect pest; he stirs up trouble among Jews the world over, and is a ringleader of the Nazarene sect. [6]He has even attempted to profane the Temple. We placed him under arrest intending to judge him according to our law, [7]but the tribune Lysias intervened and took him out of our hands by force, [8]ordering his accusers to appear before you; if you ask him[a]

---

[a] Lysias.

you can find out for yourself the truth of all our accusations against this man.' ⁹The Jews supported him, asserting that these were the facts. ¹⁰When the governor motioned him to speak, Paul answered:

Paul's speech before the Roman governor

'I know that you have administered justice over this nation for many years, and I can therefore speak with confidence in my defence. ¹¹As you can verify for yourself, it is no more than twelve days since I went up to Jerusalem on pilgrimage, ¹²and it is not true that they ever found me arguing with anyone or stirring up the mob, either in the Temple, in the synagogues, or about the town; neither can they prove any of ¹³the accusations they are making against me now. ¹⁴What I do admit to you is this: it is according to the Way which they describe as a sect that I worship the God of my ancestors, retaining my belief in all points of the Law and in what is written in the prophets; ¹⁵and I hold the same hope in God as they do that there will be a resurrection of good men and bad men alike. ¹⁶In these things, I, as much as they, do my best to keep a clear conscience at all times before God and man. ¹⁷After several years I came to bring alms to my nation and to make offerings; ¹⁸it was in connection with these that they found me in the Temple; I had been purified, and there was no crowd involved, and no disturbance. ¹⁹But some Jews from Asia... - these are the ones who should have appeared before you and accused me of whatever they had against me. ²⁰At least let those who are present say what crime they found me guilty of when I stood before the Sanhedrin, ²¹unless it were to do with this single outburst, when I stood up among them and called out: It is about the resurrection of the dead that I am on trial before you today.'

Paul's captivity at Caesarea

²²At this, Felix, who knew more about the Way than most people, adjourned the case, saying, 'When Lysias the tribune has come down I will go into your case'. ²³He then gave orders to the centurion that Paul should be kept under arrest but free from restriction, and that none of his own people should be prevented from seeing to his needs. ²⁴Some days later Felix came with his wife Drusilla who was a Jewess.ᵇ ²⁴He sent for Paul and gave him a hearing on the subject of faith in Christ Jesus. ²⁵But when he began to treat of righteousness, self-control and the coming Judgement, Felix took fright and said, 'You may go for the present; I will send for you when I find it convenient'. ²⁶At the same time he had hopes of receiving money from Paul, and for this reason he sent for him frequently and had talks with him. ²⁷When the two yearsᶜ came to an end,

---

²⁴ᵇ. Youngest daughter of Herod Agrippa.

²⁴ᶜ. The maximum length of protective custody; Felix was breaking the law by continuing to detain Paul.

Felix was succeeded by Porcius Festus and, being anxious to gain favour with the Jews, Felix left Paul in custody.

Paul appeals to Caesar

25 [1]Three days after his arrival in the province, Festus went up to Jerusalem from Caeserea. [2]The chief priests and leaders of the Jews informed him of the case against Paul, urgently [3]asking him to support them rather than Paul, and to have him transferred to Jerusalem. They were, in fact, preparing an ambush to murder him on the way. [4]But Festus replied that Paul would remain in custody in Caesarea, and that he would be going back there shortly himself. [5]'Let your authorities come down with me' he said 'and if there is anything wrong about the man, they can bring a charge against him.' [6]After staying with them for eight or ten days at the most, he went down to Caesarea and the next day he took his seat on the tribunal and had Paul brought in. [7]As soon as Paul appeared, the Jews who had come down from Jerusalem surrounded him, making many serious accusations which they were unable to substantiate. [8]Paul's defence was this, 'I have committed no offence whatever against either Jewish law, or the Temple, or Caesar'. [9]Festus was anxious to gain favour with the Jews, so he said to Paul, 'Are you willing to go up to Jerusalem and be tried on these charges before me there?' [10]But Paul replied, 'I am standing before the tribunal of Caesar and this is where I should be tried. I

have done the Jews no wrong, as you very well know. [11]If I am guilty of committing any capital crime, I do not ask to be spared the death penalty. But if there is no substance in the accusations these persons bring against me, no one has a right to surrender me to them. I appeal to Caesar.' [12]Then Festus conferred with his advisers and replied, 'You have appealed to Caesar; to Caesar you shall go'.

Paul appears before King Agrippa

[13]Some days later King Agrippa and Bernice[a] arrived in Caesarea and paid their respects to Festus. [14]Their visit lasted several days, and Festus put Paul's case before the king. 'There is a man here' he said 'whom Felix left behind in custody, [15]and while I was in Jerusalem the chief priests and elders of the Jews laid information against him, demanding his condemnation. [16]But I told them that Romans are not in the habit of surrendering any man, until the accused confronts his accusers and is given an opportunity to defend himself against the charge. [17]So they came here with me, and I wasted no time but took my seat on the tribunal the very next day and had the man brought in. [18]When confronted with him, his accusers did not charge him with any of the crimes I had expected; [19]but they had some argument or other with him about their own religion and about a dead man called Jesus whom

---

[25] a. Agrippa, Bernice and Drusilla (24:24) were children of Herod Agrippa I.

Paul alleged to be alive. ²⁰Not feeling qualified to deal with questions of this sort, I asked him if he would be willing to go to Jerusalem to be tried there on this issue. ²¹But Paul put in an appeal for his case to be reserved for the judgement of the august emperor, so I ordered him to be remanded until I could send him to Caesar.' ²²Agrippa said to Festus, 'I should like to hear the man myself'. 'Tomorrow' he answered 'you shall hear him.' ²³So the next day Agrippa and Bernice arrived in great state and entered the audience chamber attended by the tribunes and the city notables; and Festus ordered Paul to be brought in. ²⁴Then Festus said, 'King Agrippa, and all here present with us, you see before you the man about whom the whole Jewish community has petitioned me, both in Jerusalem and here, loudly protesting that he ought not to be allowed to remain alive. ²⁵For my own part I am satisfied that he has committed no capital crime, but when he himself appealed to the august emperor I decided to send him. ²⁶But I have nothing definite that I can write to his Imperial Majesty about him; that is why I have produced him before you all, and before you in particular, King Agrippa, so that after the examination I may have something to write. ²⁷It seems to me pointless to send a prisoner without indicating the charges against him.'

26 ¹Then Agrippa said to Paul, 'You have leave to speak on your own behalf'. And Paul held up his hand and began his defence:

Paul's speech before King Agrippa

²'I consider myself fortunate, King Agrippa, in that it is before you I am to answer today all the charges made against me by the Jews, ³the more so because you are an expert in matters of custom and controversy among the Jews. So I beg you to listen to me patiently. ⁴My manner of life from my youth, a life spent from the beginning among my own people and in Jerusalem, is common knowledge among the Jews. ⁵They have known me for a long time and could testify, if they would, that I followed the strictest party in our religion and lived as a Pharisee. ⁶And now it is for my hope in the promise made by God to our ancestors that I am on trial, ⁷the promise that our twelve tribes, constant in worship night and day, hope to attain. For that hope, Sire, I am actually put on trial by Jews! ⁸Why does it seem incredible to you that God should raise the dead? ⁹As for me, I once thought it was my duty to use every means to oppose the name of Jesus the Nazarene. ¹⁰This I did in Jerusalem; I myself threw many of the saints into prison, acting on authority from the chief priests, and when they were sentenced to death I cast my vote against them. ¹¹I often went round the synagogues inflicting penalties, trying in this way to force them to renounce their faith; my fury against them was so extreme that I even pursued them into foreign cities. ¹²On one such expedition I was going to Damascus, armed with full powers and a commission from the chief priests,

[13]and at midday as I was on my way, your Majesty, I saw a light brighter than the sun come down from heaven. It shone brilliantly round me and my fellow travellers. [14]We all fell to the ground, and I heard a voice saying to me in Hebrew, "Saul, Saul, why are you persecuting me? It is hard for you, kicking like this against the goad."[a] [15]Then I said: Who are you, Lord? And the Lord answered, "I am Jesus, and you are persecuting me. [16]But get up and stand on your feet, for I have appeared to you for this reason: to appoint you as my servant and as witness of this vision in which you have seen me, and of others in which I shall appear to you. [17]I shall deliver you from the people and from the pagans, to whom I am sending you [18]to open their eyes, so that they may turn from darkness to light,[b] from the dominion of Satan to God, and receive, through faith in me, forgiveness of their sins and a share in the inheritance of the sanctified." [19]After that, King Agrippa, I could not disobey the heavenly vision. [20]On the contrary I started preaching, first to the people of Damascus, then to those of Jerusalem and all the countryside of Judaea, and also to the pagans, urging them to repent and turn to God, proving their change of heart by their deeds. [21]This was why the Jews laid hands on me in the Temple and tried to do away with me. [22]But I was blessed with God's help, and so I have stood firm to this day, testifying to great

---

[26a.] Greek proverbial expression for useless resistance.
[26b.] Quotations from Jr 1; Is 42; Is 9.

and small alike, saying nothing more than what the prophets and Moses himself said would happen: ²³that the Christ was to suffer and that, as the first to rise from the dead, he was to proclaim that light now shone for our people and for the pagans too.'

His hearers' reactions

²⁴He had reached this point in his defence when Festus shouted out, 'Paul, you are out of your mind; all that learning of yours is driving you mad'. ²⁵'Festus, your Excellency,' answered Paul 'I am not mad: I am speaking nothing but the sober truth. ²⁶The king understands these matters, and to him I now speak with assurance, confident that nothing of all this is lost on him; after all, these things were not done in a corner. ²⁷King Agrippa, do you believe in the prophets? I know you do.' ²⁸At this Agrippa said to Paul, 'A little more, and your arguments would make a Christian of me'. ²⁹'Little or more,' Paul replied 'I wish before God that not only you but all who have heard me today would come to be as I am - except for these chains.' ³⁰At this the king rose to his feet, with the governor and Bernice and those who sat there with them. ³¹When they had retired they talked together and agreed, 'This man is doing nothing that deserves death or imprisonment'. ³²And Agrippa remarked to Festus, 'The man could have been set free if he had not appealed to Caesar'.

The departure for Rome

27 [1]When it had been decided that we should sail for Italy, Paul and some other prisoners were handed over to a centurion called Julius, of the Augustan cohort. [2]We boarded a vessel from Adramyttium bound for ports on the Asiatic coast, and put to sea; we had Aristatchus with us, a Macedonian of Thessalonika. [3]Next day we put in at Sidon, and Julius was considerate enough to allow Paul to go to his friends to be looked after. [4]From there we put to sea again, but as the winds were against us we sailed under the lee of Cyprus, [5]then across the open sea off Cilicia and Pamphylia taking a fortnight to reach Myra in Lycia. [6]There the centurion found an Alexandrian ship leaving for Italy and put us aboard. [7]For some days we made little headway, and we had difficulty in making Cnidus. The wind would not allow us to touch there, so we sailed under the lee of Crete off Cape Salmone [8]and struggled along the coast until we came to a place called Fair Havens, near the town of Lasea.

Storm and shipwreck

[9]A great deal of time had been lost, and navigation was already hazardous since it was now well after the time of the Fast,[a] so Paul gave them this warning, [10]'Friends, I can see this voyage will be dangerous and that we run the risk

---

27 a. 'The Fast', the feast of Atonement, was kept about the time of the autumn equinox; winter was coming on.

of losing not only the cargo and the ship but also our lives as well'. [11]But the centurion took more notice of the captain and the ship's owner than of what Paul was saying; [12]and since the harbour was unsuitable for wintering, the majority were for putting out from there in the hope of wintering at Phoenix - a harbour in Crete, facing south-west and north-west. [13]A southerly breeze sprang up and, thinking their objective as good as reached, they weighed anchor and began to sail past Crete, close inshore. [14]But it was not long before a hurricane, the 'north-easter' as they call it, burst on them from across the island. [15]The ship was caught and could not be turned head-on to the wind, so we had to give way to it and let ourselves be driven. [16]We ran under the lee of a small island called Cauda and managed with some difficulty to bring the ship's boat under control. [17]They hoisted it aboard and with the help of tackle bound cables round the ship; then, afraid of running aground on the Syrtis banks, they floated out the sea-anchor and so let themselves drift. [18]As we were making very heavy weather of it, the next day they began to jettison the cargo, [19]and the third day they threw the ship's gear overboard with their own hands. [20]For a number of days both the sun and the stars were invisible and the storm raged unabated until at last we gave up all hope of surviving. [21]Then, when they had been without food for a long time, Paul stood up among the men. 'Friends,' he said 'if you had listened to me and not put out from Crete, you would have spared yourselves all this damage and loss. 22But now I ask you not to give way to despair. There will be no loss of life at all, only of the ship. 23Last night there was standing beside me an angel of the God to whom I belong and whom I serve, 24and he said, "Do not be afraid, Paul. You are destined to appear before Caesar, and for this reason God grants you the safety of all who are sailing with you." 25So take courage, friends; I trust in God that things will turn out just as I was told; 26but we are to be stranded on some island.' 27On the fourteenth night we were being driven one way and another in the Adriatic,[b] when about midnight the crew sensed that land of some sort was near. 28They took soundings and found twenty fathoms; after a short interval they sounded again and found fifteen fathoms. 29Then, afraid that we might run aground somewhere on a reef, they dropped four anchors from the stern and prayed for daylight. 30When some of the crew tried to escape from the ship and lowered the ship's boat into the sea as though to lay out anchors from the bows, 31Paul said to the centurion and his men, 'Unless those men stay on board you cannot hope to be saved'. 32So the soldiers cut the boat's ropes and let it drop away. 33Just before daybreak Paul urged them all to have something to eat. 'For fourteen days' he

---

27 b. The term includes the seas between Greece, Italy and Africa.

said 'you have been in suspense, going hungry and eating nothing. ³⁴Let me persuade you to have something to eat; your safety is not in doubt. Not a hair of your heads will be lost.' ³⁵With these words he took some bread, gave thanks to God in front of them all, broke it and began to eat. ³⁶Then they all plucked up courage and took something to eat themselves. ³⁷We were in all two hundred and seventy-six souls on board that ship. ³⁸When they had eaten what they wanted they lightened the ship by throwing the corn overboard into the sea. ³⁹When day came they did not recognise the land, but they could make out a kind of bay with a beach; they planned to run the ship aground on this if they could. ⁴⁰They slipped the anchors and left them to the sea, and at the same time loosened the lashings of the rudders; then, hoisting the foresail to the wind, they headed for the beach. ⁴¹But the cross-currents carried them into a shoal and the vessel ran aground. The bows were wedged in and stuck fast, while the stern began to break up with the pounding of the waves. ⁴²The soldiers planned to kill the prisoners for fear that any should swim off and escape. ⁴³But the centurion was determined to bring Paul safely through, and would not let them do what they intended. He gave orders that those who could swim should jump overboard first and so get ashore, ⁴⁴and the rest follow either on planks or on pieces of wreckage. In this way all came safe and sound to land.

Waiting in Malta

28 ¹Once we had come safely through, we discovered that the island was called Malta. ²The inhabitants treated us with unusual kindness. They made us all welcome, and they lit a huge fire because it had started to rain and the weather was cold. ³Paul had collected a bundle of sticks and was putting them on the fire when a viper brought out by the heat attached itself to his hand. ⁴When the natives saw the creature hanging from his hand they said to one another, 'That man must be a murderer; he may have escaped the sea, but divine vengeance would not let him live'. ⁵However, he shook the creature off into the fire and came to no harm, ⁶although they were expecting him at any moment to swell up or drop dead on the spot. After they had waited a long time without seeing anything out of the ordinary happen to him, they changed their minds and began to say he was a god. ⁷In that neighbourhood there were estates belonging to the prefect of the island, whose name was Publius. He received us and entertained us hospitably for three days. ⁸It so happened that Publius' father was in bed, suffering from feverish attacks and dysentery. Paul went in to see him, and after a prayer he laid his hands on the man and healed him. ⁹When this happened, the other sick people on the island came as well and were cured; ¹⁰they honoured us with many marks of respect, and when we sailed they put on board the provisions we needed.

From Malta to Rome

[11]At the end of three months we set sail in a ship that had wintered in the island; she came from Alexandria and her figurehead was the Twins. [12]We put in at Syracuse and spent three days there; [13]from there we followed the coast up to Rhegium. After one day there a south wind sprang up and on the second day we made Puteoli,[a] [14]where we found some brothers and were much rewarded by staying a week with them. And so we came to Rome. [15]When the brothers there heard of our arrival they came to meet us, as far as the Forum of Appius and the Three Taverns. When Paul saw them he thanked God and took courage. [16]On our arrival in Rome Paul was allowed to stay in lodgings of his own with the soldier who guarded him.

Paul makes contact with the Roman Jews

[17]After three days he called together the leading Jews. When they had assembled, he said to them, 'Brothers, although I have done nothing against our people or the customs of our ancestors, I was arrested in Jerusalem and handed over to the Romans. [18]They examined me and would have set me free, since they found me guilty of nothing involving the death penalty; [19]but the Jews lodged an objection, and I was forced to appeal to Caesar, not that I had any accusation to make against my own nation. [20]That is why I have asked to see you and talk to you, for

---

[28 a.] Pozzuoli, on the Gulf of Naples.

it is on account of the hope of Israel that I wear this chain.' [21]They answered, 'We have received no letters from Judaea about you, nor has any countryman of yours arrived here with any report or story of anything to your discredit. [22]We think it would be as well to hear your own account of your position; all we know about this sect is that opinion everywhere condemns it.'

Paul's declaration to the Roman Jews

[23]So they arranged a day with him and a large number of them visited him at his lodgings. He put his case to them, testifying to the kingdom of God and trying to persuade them about Jesus, arguing from the Law of Moses and the prophets. This went on from early morning until evening, [24]and some were convinced by what he said, while the rest were sceptical. [25]So they disagreed among themselves and, as they went away, Paul had one last thing to say to them, 'How aptly the Holy Spirit spoke when he told your ancestors through the prophet Isaiah: [26]"Go to this nation and say: You will hear and hear again but not understand, see and see again, but not perceive. [27]For the heart of this nation has grown coarse, their ears are dull of hearing and they have shut their eyes, for fear they should see with their eyes, hear with their ears, understand with their heart, and be converted and be healed by me."[b] [28]Understand,

---

[28 b.] Is 6:9-10

then, that this salvation of God has been sent to the pagans; they will listen to it.'

Epilogue

[30]Paul spent the whole of the two years[c] in his own rented lodging. He welcomed all who came to visit him, [31]proclaiming the kingdom of God and teaching the truth about the Lord Jesus Christ with complete freedom and without hindrance from anyone.

[28 c.] See note on 24:27